ROUGH GUIDES

T0012638

POCKET **ROUGH GUIDE**
VENICE

this edition updated by
ROS BELFORD

PAX EVAN
TIBI GELI
MAR STA
CE MEVS

CONTENTS

VENICE

Founded 1,500 years ago on a cluster of mudflats in the centre of the lagoon, Venice rose to become Europe's main trading post between the West and the East, and at its height controlled an empire that extended from the Dolomites to Cyprus. The fabric of the present-day city, astonishingly well preserved, bears testimony to Venice's former grandeur in virtually every square and street.

Venetian gondolier punting gondola through the green canal waters of Venice

View of the iconic Venice gondolas, the church of San Giorgio Maggiore in the background

In the heyday of the Venetian Republic, some two hundred thousand people lived in Venice, three times its present population. Merchants from Europe and western Asia maintained warehouses here; transactions in the banks and bazaars of the Rialto dictated the value of commodities all over the continent; in the dockyards of the Arsenale the workforce was so vast that a warship could be built and fitted out in a single day; and the Piazza San Marco was thronged with people here to set up deals or report to the Republic's government. Nowadays it's no longer a buzzing metropolis but rather the embodiment of a fabulous past, dependent for its survival largely on the people who come to marvel at its relics.

The monuments that draw the largest crowds are the Basilica di San Marco – the mausoleum of the city's patron saint – and the Palazzo Ducale or Doge's Palace. Certainly these are the most imposing structures in the city, but a roll-call of the churches worth visiting would feature more than a dozen names. Many of the city's treasures remain in the churches for which they were created, but a sizeable number have been removed to one or other of Venice's museums, with the Accademia holding the lion's share. This cultural heritage is a source of endless fascination, but you should also discard your itineraries for a day and just wander

Best place for a picnic

The beauty of the cityscape and the price of restaurants make picnicking an enticing proposition in Venice – but there are strict by-laws against picnics in the city squares. So buy provisions at Rialto market then hop on a vaporetto to Giardini (see page 97), or to the Biennale Gardens where you'll find shade, a bit of greenery, and a fabulous panorama of Venice and the lagoon.

When to visit

Venice's tourist season is very nearly an all-year affair. Peak season, when hotel rooms are difficult to come by at short notice, is from **April to October**; try to avoid **July and August**, when the climate becomes oppressively hot and clammy. The other two popular spells are the **Carnevale** (leading up to Lent) and the weeks on each side of **Christmas**.

For the ideal combination of comparative peace and a mild climate, the two or three weeks **immediately preceding Easter** are perhaps best. **November and December** are somewhat less reliable: some days bring fogs that make it difficult to see from one bank of the Canal Grande to the other. If you want to see the city at its quietest, **January** is the month to go – take plenty of warm clothes, though, as the winds off the Adriatic can be savage, and you should be prepared for floods throughout the winter. This **acqua alta**, as Venice's seasonal flooding is called, has been an element of Venetian life for centuries, but nowadays it's far more frequent than it used to be: between October and late February it's not uncommon for flooding to occur several days in succession.

– the anonymous parts of Venice reveal as much of the city as its well-known attractions.

The historic centre of Venice is made up of 118 islands, tied together by some four hundred bridges to form an amalgamation that's divided into six large administrative districts known as *sestieri*, three on each side of the Canal Grande.

Versace store in Venice

461

Where to...

Shop

The main retail zones in Venice are the **Mercerie** (north of Piazza San Marco) and **Calle Larga XXII Marzo** (west of the Piazza). Nowadays, they are dominated by famous Italian brands such as Gucci, Prada and Trussardi. In quieter parts of the city, notably in San Polo, some authentically Venetian outlets and workshops are still in operation. The manufacture of exquisite decorative papers is a distinctively Venetian skill; small craft studios continue to produce beautiful handmade bags and shoes; and lots of shops sell glass, lace and Carnival masks – the quintessential souvenir, though read labels carefully as many are cheap copies made thousands of miles from Venice. The website ⓦ veneziaautentica.com is an excellent place to find genuine craftspeople and shops selling authentic work by locals.
OUR FAVOURITES: Archimede Seguso, see page 33; Daniela Ghezzo Segalin, see page 38; Goldoni, see page 38.

Eat and drink

Near the Piazza, restaurant quality is generally poor and prices inflated. However, out in the quieter zones Venice has an increasing number of excellent **restaurants**. Three interesting, slightly off-the-beaten-track areas to head for are Santa Croce, Castello, in the area between San Giorgio and the Arsenale, northern Cannaregio along the Fondamente Misericordia and Ormesini, the studenty area in the west of Dorsoduro, and Via Garibaldi in Sant'Elena. Here, it is still possible to find homely trattorias where you can eat a simple pasta or main with a glass of wine for under €20. One of the most appealing aspects of Venetian social life is captured in the phrase "*andemo a ombra*", literally an offer to go into the shade, but in fact an invitation for a drink – specifically, a glass of wine (*ombra*). An **enoteca** is a bar specializing in wines, while a **bácaro** is a **bar** that offers a range of snacks called **cicchetti**; usually €2–2.50 per portion, they may include *polpette* (small beef and garlic meatballs), *carciofini* (artichoke hearts) and *polipi* (baby octopus or squid). Many *bácari* also produce main dishes, such as risotto or seafood pasta. Excellent food is also served at many **osterie**, the simplest of which have just a few tables. Restaurants often have a separate street-side bar.
OUR FAVOURITES: Al Bacareto, see page 46; Ai Quattro Feri, see page 60; Da Fiore, see page 46.

Party

Venice is notorious for its lack of **nightlife**, but there are a good number of late-opening bars with live music and DJs, though venues tend to be small and there are strict by-laws against late-night noise. The best of these are in Dorsoduro. However, music in Venice, to all intents and purposes, means classical music – the top-bracket **music venues** are La Fenice, the Teatro Malibran and the Teatro Goldoni, all in the San Marco *sestiere*, but there are frequent concerts in churches (most often of Vivaldi) and an annual programme of romantic French music in the Palazzo Bru Zane in San Polo.
OUR FAVOURITES: Al Parlamento, see page 84; Café Noir, see page 61; Margaret DuChamp, see page 61.

Venice at a glance

The Canal Grande p.100.
Venice's high street, dividing the city in two. Taking a vaporetto along it is an essential part of any visit to the city.

Cannaregio p.74.
Tranquil and untouristy district. The long, northern quaysides are dotted with excellent places for eating and drinking.

San Polo and Santa Croce p.62.
Two quarters riddled with intricate alleyways and little squares – and the famous Rialto market.

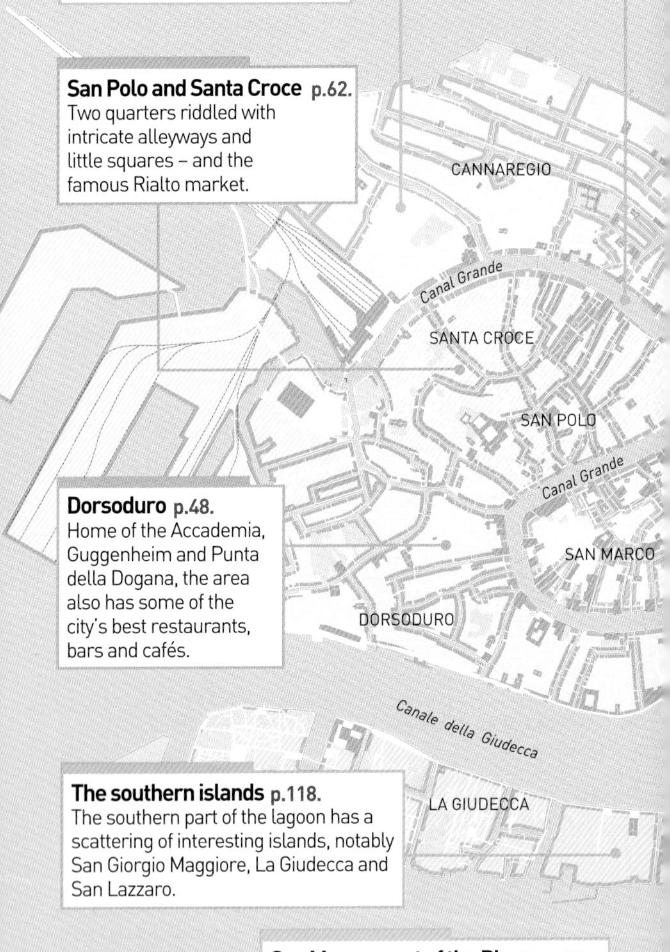

CANNAREGIO

Canal Grande

SANTA CROCE

SAN POLO

Canal Grande

SAN MARCO

Dorsoduro p.48.
Home of the Accademia, Guggenheim and Punta della Dogana, the area also has some of the city's best restaurants, bars and cafés.

DORSODURO

Canale della Giudecca

The southern islands p.118.
The southern part of the lagoon has a scattering of interesting islands, notably San Giorgio Maggiore, La Giudecca and San Lazzaro.

LA GIUDECCA

San Marco: west of the Piazza p.40.
Calle Larga XXII Marzo to the west of the Piazza is the place to find the big Italian designer names.

San Marco: north of the Piazza p.34.
The Mercerie – the chain of streets linking
the Piazza to the Rialto Bridge – is Venice's
busiest shopping district.

The northern islands p.108.
San Michele is the city's cemetery;
the glassmaking island of Murano is
close, while in the outermost reaches
lie Burano and Torcello.

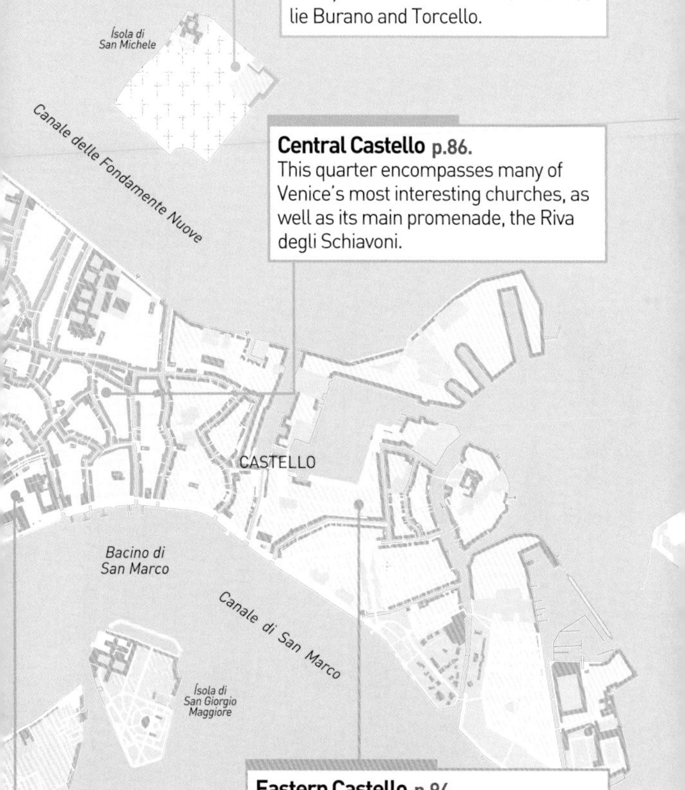

*Ísola di
San Michele*

Canale delle Fondamente Nuove

Central Castello p.86.
This quarter encompasses many of
Venice's most interesting churches, as
well as its main promenade, the Riva
degli Schiavoni.

CASTELLO

*Bacino di
San Marco*

Canale di San Marco

*Ísola di
San Giorgio
Maggiore*

Eastern Castello p.94.
Sprawling area that's home to the former
industrial centre (the Arsenale) and some
of the city's grittier residential areas.

San Marco: the Piazza p.24.
The hub of the city and location of its
two prime monuments – the Palazzo
Ducale and the Basilica di San Marco.

15

Things not to miss

It's not possible to see everything Venice has to offer in one trip – and we don't suggest you try. What follows is a selective taste of the city's highlights.

< The Frari
See page 69
The gargantuan edifice of Santa Maria Gloriosa dei Frari contains masterpieces by Titian, Bellini, Donatello and many more.

∨ Torcello
See page 112
The majestic cathedral of Torcello – the oldest building in the whole lagoon – marks the spot where the lagoon city came into existence.

< **The Palazzo Ducale**
See page 27
The home of the doges was the nerve-centre of the entire Venetian empire, and was decorated by some of the greatest Venetian artists.

∨ **Burano**
See page 110
The brightly painted exteriors of the houses of Burano give this island an appearance that's distinct from any other settlement in the lagoon.

∧ San Michele
See page 108
Located a short distance north of the city centre, San Michele is possibly the most beautiful cemetery in the world.

‹ Murano
See page 109
Glass has been the basis of Murano's economy for seven hundred years, and there are still plenty of factories where you can admire the glassblowers' amazing skills.

∧ **La Giudecca**
See page 119
Once one of the city's main industrial zones, La Giudecca is nowadays a predominantly residential area that retains much of the spirit of the city prior to the age of mass tourism.

∨ **Ca' d'Oro**
See page 79
Once the most extravagant house on the Canal Grande, the Ca' d'Oro today is home to an engagingly miscellaneous art collection.

△ **Punta della Dogana**
See page 50
The Pinault Collection is a stunner – installed in the dazzlingly revamped customs house, this is Europe's largest display of contemporary art.

◁ **Museo Correr**
See page 30
Now joined to the Libreria Sansoviniana and the archeological museum, the Correr is a museum of Venetian history with an excellent art gallery upstairs.

< **The Guggenheim**
See page 49

For a break from the Renaissance, spend an hour or two with the Guggenheim's fine array of modern art.

∨ **Ca' Rezzonico**
See page 57

Devoted to the visual and applied arts of the eighteenth century, the Ca' Rezzonico contains several wonderful paintings and some frankly bizarre furniture.

THINGS NOT TO MISS

Day One in Venice

Basilica di San Marco. See page 24. Begin at the heart of the city, the Piazza San Marco and the Basilica – and get here early, before the queues for the cathedral build up.

Coffee. See page 33. Splash out just once on a coffee at one of the Piazza's famous cafés.

Palazzo Ducale. See page 27. Explore the Doge's Palace, a vast and fascinating building, which will take up most of the rest of the morning.

Basilica di San Marco

Lunch. Ramble west, away from the Piazza itself, to *Al Bacareto* (see page 46), which has been going for decades, and is always dependable.

Santo Stefano and Santa Maria del Giglio. See pages 41 and 43. Loop back towards the Piazza, dropping in at these two churches, and maybe window-shopping on Calle Larga XXII Marzo, the most upmarket street in the city.

Correr museum, Libreria and archeological museum. See page 30. The rambling Correr museum gives you some essential historical background – and it has a fine art gallery and archeological museum.

Coffee at Rosa Salva

Dinner. From the Piazza, saunter along the shopping streets of the Mercerie (see page 34), as a prelude to crossing the Rialto Bridge for an aperitivo and dinner in the market district (see page 62), where you'll find some atmospheric local bars.

Campo Cesare Battisti, San Polo

Day Two in Venice

The Accademia. See page 48. The city's main art gallery – one of Europe's great collections – and worth several hours of your time.

Salute and the Záttere. See page 51. Visit the great church of the Salute, en route to the Záttere, where the views are fantastic.

San Trovaso. See page 53. Strike north from Záttere and look in on the oldest remaining gondola workshop in the city.

Lunch. Head to Campo di Santa Margherita (see page 55), a buzzing square where you can revive yourself at one of its many bars and cafés.

The Tempest by Giorgione, the Accademia

The Frari. See page 69. Continue north from Campo di Santa Margherita to the city's mightiest Gothic church, which features a couple of first-rate works by Titian.

Scuola Grande di San Rocco. See page 70. The Scuola features a stupendous cycle of Tintoretto paintings.

San Zanipolo. See page 86. Stroll to Piazzale Roma, then take the #5.2 vaporetto to Fondamente Nove, which is close to the city's other gargantuan church, San Zanipolo (Santi Giovanni e Paolo).

Traditional Venetian gondolas

Drinks. From Zanipolo you can wander westward into Cannaregio; the bars and restaurants of northern Cannaregio are among the best in Venice – *Anice Stellato* (see page 83) is a particular favourite.

Anice Stellato

Off the beaten track

To get a feel for genuine Venice, you'll need to explore the peripheries of the city, where you'll find some atmospheric quarters and intriguing sights.

San Sebastiano and Angelo Raffaele. See page 54. These neighbouring churches make a great start to a day in Venice's less touristed zones.

San Nicolò dei Mendicoli. See page 55. Now walk to the western edge of Dorsoduro and the ancient church of San Nicolò dei Mendicoli.

Tolentini. See page 71. Stroll along the canal north from here and you'll be heading in the right direction for the Tolentini church; the Giardino Padadopoli is also close at hand, and a good spot for a sit down.

San Sebastiano church

Lunch. In Campo Sant'Anzolo Raffaele, *Trattoria Anzolo Raffaele* (see page 61) is a terrific spot for a fine lunch of seasonal dishes made of locally-sourced ingredients with an excellent glass of wine.

The Ghetto. See page 75. From nearby Piazzale Roma, the #4.2 and #5.2 will take you to Guglie, the nearest stop to the Ghetto.

Madonna dell'Orto. See page 78. A short way north of the Ghetto, you'll find Tintoretto's parish church, one of the most beautiful in Venice.

San Pietro. See page 97. From the Madonna dell'Orto stop, take the #5.2 all the way to San Pietro, where the city's former cathedral nestles amid boatyards.

Water canal in the Jewish Ghetto

Dinner. The #5.2 continues over to the Lido, then bounces back, via Sant'Elena, to Giardini. For dinner you could choose between two of the very best restaurants in the city: *Corte Sconta* or *Al Covo* (see page 99).

Corte Sconta

On the water

One long boat-trip is absolutely essential for any visit to Venice. Arm yourself with a travel pass, and head out to some of the further-flung islands.

Torcello. See page 112. The hour-long voyage out to the island of Torcello, where the settlement of the lagoon began, is a treat in itself, and the ancient cathedral is a magnificent thing. Be sure to climb the belltower.

Burano. See page 110. On your way back, get off at the lace-making island of Burano for an hour or so.

Murano. See page 109. And then jump back on board for Murano and its glass factories.

Lunch. Eat at Burano's Michelin-starred *Venissa* or its simpler sister, the *Osteria Contemporanea* (see page 116). Or wait until you get to Murano and head for the refined *Punta Conterie* (see page 116).

San Zaccaria. See page 90. From Murano the #4.2 goes all the way to San Zaccaria – its waterlogged crypt brings home just how perilous the city's relationship with the water is.

The Arsenale. See page 96. Take a look at the former powerhouse of the Venetian economy.

San Giorgio Maggiore. See page 118. Take the #2 over to San Giorgio Maggiore, not just for its architecture and paintings, but for the superb panorama from the top of its campanile.

La Giudecca. See page 119. Hop back on the #2 for one stop to reach La Giudecca. There's one great building here – the Redentore – but most of the island is a residential district, with boatyards along its southern shore.

The Canal Grande. See page 138. End the day with a night-time voyage down the city's main thoroughfare, on the unhurried #1 or #N vaporetto.

Burano island

Canal Grande from Rialto Bridge

The Arsenale entrance

PLACES

Piazza San Marco

San Marco: the Piazza

The *sestiere* of San Marco – a rectangle smaller than 1000m by 500m – has been the nucleus of Venice from the start of the city's existence. The Piazza San Marco was where the first rulers built their citadel – the Palazzo Ducale – and it was here that they established their most important church – the Basilica di San Marco. Over the succeeding centuries the Basilica evolved into the most ostentatiously rich church in Christendom, and the Palazzo Ducale grew to accommodate and celebrate Venice's system of government. Meanwhile, the setting for these two great edifices developed into a public space so dignified that no other square in the city was thought fit to bear the name "piazza" – all other Venetian squares are campi or campielli. Nowadays the San Marco area is home to the city's plushest hotels, while elegant and exorbitant cafés spill out onto the pavement from the Piazza's arcades, and the swankiest shops in Venice line the streets that radiate from it.

The Basilica di San Marco

MAP P.26, POCKET MAP G14–H14
Ⓦ basilicasanmarco.it. Charge, but free entry for prayer via the Porta dei Fiori on the Piazzetta dei Leoncini.

All over Venice you see images of the lion of St Mark holding a book on which is carved the text "Pax tibi, Marce evangelista meus. Hic requiescet corpus tuum" ("Peace

The magnificent golden ceiling of the Basilica di San Marco

The government of Venice

Virtually from the beginning, the **government of Venice** was dominated by the merchant class, who in 1297 enacted a measure known as the **Serrata del Maggior Consiglio** (Closure of the Great Council). From then onwards, any man not belonging to one of the wealthy families on the list compiled for the *Serrata* was ineligible to participate in the running of the city. After a while, this list was succeeded by a register of patrician births and marriages called the **Libro d'Oro**, upon which all claims to membership of the elite were based. By the second decade of the fourteenth century, the constitution of Venice had reached a form that was to endure until the coming of Napoleon; its civil and criminal code, defined in the early thirteenth century, was equally resistant to change.

What made the political system stable was its web of counterbalancing councils and committees, and its exclusion of any youngsters. Most patricians entered the Maggior Consiglio at 25 and could not expect a middle-ranking post before 45; from the middle ranks to the top was another long haul – the average age of the doge from 1400 to 1600 was 72.

The **doge** was the figurehead of the Republic rather than anything akin to its president, and numerous restrictions were placed on his activities – all his letters were read by censors, for example. On the other hand, whereas his colleagues on the various state councils were elected for terms as brief as a month, the doge was **elected for life** and sat on all the major councils, which at the very least made him extremely influential.

be with you Mark, my Evangelist. Here shall your body rest"). These supposedly are the words with which St Mark was greeted by an angel who appeared to him on the night he took shelter in the lagoon on his way back to Rome. Having thus assured themselves of the sacred ordination of their city, the first Venetians duly went about fulfilling the angelic prophecy. In 828 two merchants stole the body of St Mark from its tomb in Alexandria and brought it back to Venice. Work began immediately on a shrine to house him, and the Basilica di San Marco was consecrated in 832. The amazing church you see today is essentially the version built in 1063–94, embellished in the succeeding centuries. When you visit, large bags must be left, free of charge, at nearby Calle San Basso 315a. To avoid queues, get here about half an hour before it opens.

The exterior

The marble-clad exterior is adorned with numerous pieces of ancient stonework, but a couple of features warrant special attention: the **Romanesque carvings** of the arches of the central doorway; and the group of porphyry figures set into the wall on the waterfront side – known as the **Tetrarchs**, in all likelihood they're a fourth-century Egyptian work depicting Diocletian and his three co-rulers of the then unravelling Roman Empire.

The real **horses of San Marco** are inside the church – the four outside are modern replicas. On the main facade, the only ancient mosaic to survive is *The Arrival of the Body of St Mark*, above the **Porta di Sant'Alipio** (far left); made around 1260, it features the earliest known image of the Basilica.

Just inside, the intricately patterned stonework of the **narthex floor** is mostly eleventh- and twelfth-century, while the majority of the **mosaics** on the domes and arches constitute a series of Old Testament scenes dating from the thirteenth century.

On the right of the main door from the narthex into the body of the church is a steep staircase up to the **Museo Marciano** and the **Loggia dei Cavalli** (charge), home of the fabled horses. Thieved from Constantinople in 1204, the horses are almost certainly Roman works of the second century, and are the only *quadriga* (group of four horses harnessed to a chariot) to have survived from the classical world. The scratches and the partial gilding on the horses' skin are original, added in order to catch the sunlight.

The interior

With its undulating floor of patterned marble and 4000 square metres of mosaics, the interior of the Basilica is the most opulent of any cathedral in Europe. Officially the remains of St Mark lie in the sarcophagus underneath the high altar, at the back of which you can see the most precious of San Marco's treasures, the astonishing **Pala d'Oro** (charge) – the "golden altar screen". Commissioned in 976 in Constantinople, the *Pala* was enlarged, enriched and rearranged by Byzantine goldsmiths in 1105, then by Venetians in 1209 to incorporate some of the less cumbersome loot from the Fourth Crusade, and again (finally) in 1345. Tucked into the corner of the south transept is the door of the **treasury** (charge), which includes an unsurpassed collection of Byzantine silver and gold work.

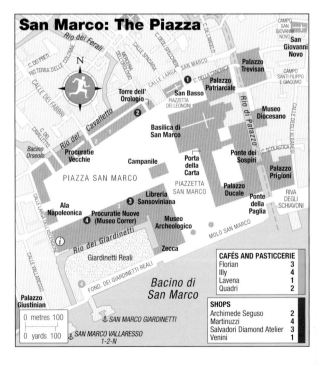

Another marvel is the **rood screen**, surmounted by marble figures of The Virgin, St Mark and the Apostles (1394) by Jacobello and Pietro Paolo Dalle Masegne. Finally, Venice's most revered religious image, the tenth-century **Icon of the Madonna of Nicopeia**, stands in the chapel on the east side of the north transept; until 1204 it was one of the most revered icons in Constantinople, where it used to be carried ceremonially at the head of the emperor's army.

The Palazzo Ducale

MAP P.26, POCKET MAP G14–H14
Ⓦ palazzoducale.visitmuve.it. Charge. Museum Pass or Piazza San Marco Museums Card.

Architecturally, the Palazzo Ducale is a unique mixture: the style of its exterior, with its geometrically patterned stonework and continuous tracery walls, can only be called Islamicized Gothic, whereas the courtyards and much of the interior are based on Classical forms – a blending of influences that led Ruskin to declare it "the central building of the world". Unquestionably, it is the finest secular building of its era in Europe, and the central building of Venice: it was the residence of the doge, the home of all of Venice's governing councils, its law courts, a sizeable number of its civil servants and even its prisons. All power in the Venetian Republic was controlled within this building.

The original doge's fortress was founded at the start of the ninth century, but it was in the fourteenth and fifteenth centuries that the Palazzo Ducale acquired its present shape. The principal entrance, the **Porta della Carta**, was commissioned in 1438 by Doge Francesco Fóscari, and is one of the most ornate Gothic works in the city. The passageway into the Palazzo ends under the **Arco Fóscari**, which you can see only after getting your ticket, as visitors

Palazzo Ducale

are nowadays directed in through the arcades on the lagoon side.

From the ticket office you're directed straight into the **Museo dell'Opera**, where the originals of most of the superb capitals from the external loggias are well displayed. From ground level you are directed up the Scala dei Censori to the upper arcade and then up the gilded **Scala d'Oro**, the main internal staircase of the Palazzo Ducale.

The state rooms

A subsidiary staircase leads to the **Doge's Apartments** (look out for Titian's small fresco of *St Christopher*), then the Scala d'Oro continues up to the *secondo piano nobile*, where you soon enter the **Anticollegio**. With its pictures by Tintoretto and Veronese, this is one of the richest rooms in the Palazzo Ducale, and no doubt made a suitable impact on the emissaries who waited here for admission to the **Sala del Collegio**, where the doge and his inner cabinet met. Ruskin maintained that in no other part of the palace could you "enter so deeply into the heart of Venice",

The Campanile

though he was referring not to the mechanics of Venetian power but to the luscious cycle of ceiling paintings by Veronese.

The **Sala del Senato** was where most major policies were determined. A motley collection of late sixteenth-century artists produced the bombastic decoration of the walls and ceiling. Paolo Veronese again appears in the **Sala del Consiglio dei Dieci**, the room in which the much-feared Council of Ten discussed matters relating to state security. The unfortunates who were summoned before the Ten had to await their grilling in the next room, the **Sala della Bussola**; in the wall is a *Bocca di Leone* (Lion's Mouth), one of the boxes into which citizens could drop denunciations for the attention of the Ten and other state bodies.

Beyond the **armoury**, the Scala dei Censori takes you back to the second floor and the **Sala del Maggior Consiglio**, the assembly hall of all the Venetian patricians eligible to participate in the running of the city. This stupendous room, with its lavish ceiling, is dominated by the immense *Paradiso*, begun at the age of 77 by Tintoretto and completed by his son Domenico. Tintoretto was also commissioned to replace the room's frieze of portraits of the first 76 doges (the series continues in the Sala dello Scrutinio), but in the event Domenico and his assistants did the work.

The prisons

A couple of rooms later, the route descends to the **Magistrato alle Leggi**, from where the Scala dei Censori leads to the **Ponte dei Sospiri** (Bridge of Sighs) and the **Prigioni** (Prisons). Built in 1600 by Antonio Contino, the bridge takes its popular name from the sighs of the prisoners who shuffled through its corridor. In reality, though, anyone passing this way had actually been let off pretty lightly. The hard cases were kept either in the sweltering **Piombi** (the Leads), under the roof of the Palazzo Ducale, or in the sodden gloom of the **Pozzi** (the Wells) in the bottom two storeys.

The Campanile

MAP P.26, POCKET MAP G14

Ⓦ visitvenezia.eu. Charge.

The Campanile began life as a combined lighthouse and belltower, and was continually modified up to 1515, the year in which the golden angel was installed on the summit. Each of its five **bells** had a distinct function: the *Marangona*, the largest, tolled the beginning and end of the working day; the *Trottiera* was a signal for members of the Maggior Consiglio to hurry along; the *Nona* rang midday; the *Mezza Terza* announced a session of the Senate; and the smallest, the *Renghiera* or *Maleficio*, gave notice of an execution. The Campanile played another part in the Venetian penal system – "persons of scandalous behaviour" ran the risk of being subjected to the *Supplizio della Cheba* (Torture of the Cage), which

The itinerari segreti

Book in advance by emailing @ prenotazionivenezia@coopculture.it

If you want to see the rooms in which the day-to-day administration of Venice took place, take the Itinerari Segreti del Palazzo Ducale, a fascinating 75-minute guided tour through a warren of offices and passageways that interlocks with the public rooms of the building.

The numerous councils and committees of Venice required a vast civil service. Roaming through the shadow-palace in which these functionaries carried out their duties, you begin to understand why the Venetian Republic aroused in many people the sort of dread a police state inspires. The tour includes the tiny rooms of the Chancellery, in which all acts of state were drafted and tabulated, then passes through the eighteenth-century hall of the Chancellery, lined with cabinets for filing state documents. From here it's onward into a high-ceilinged den where a rope hangs, as if ready for torture, between two tiny wooden cells – the idea being that their occupants, hearing the screams of the suspended victim, would need no further encouragement to talk. After these, you're led up into the roof to see the timber-lined Piombi, or prison cells, including the one from which Casanova escaped in 1775.

involved being stuck in a crate which was then hoisted up the south face of the tower. A more cheerful diversion was provided by the *Volo dell'Anzolo* or *del Turco* (Flight of the Angel or Turk), a stunt which used to be performed each year at the end of the Carnevale, in which an intrepid volunteer would slide on a rope from the top of the Campanile to the first-floor loggia of the Palazzo Ducale to present a bouquet to the doge.

But the Campanile's most dramatic contribution to the history of the city was made on July 14, 1902, the day on which, at 9.52am, it fell down. The town councillors decided that evening that the Campanile should be rebuilt "*dov'era e com'era*" (where it was and how it was), and a decade later, on St Mark's Day 1912, the new tower was opened, in all but minor details a replica of the original. At 99m, the Campanile is the tallest structure in the city, and from the top (accessed by a lift) you can make out virtually every building, but not a single canal.

The Torre dell'Orologio

MAP P.26, POCKET MAP G14
@ torreorologio.visitmuve.it. Charge.
Guided tours only booked in advance via the website.

The other tower in the Piazza, the Torre dell'Orologio (Clock Tower),

Torre dell'Orologio

The Procuratie and Piazza San Marco

was built between 1496 and 1506. Legend relates that the makers of the clock slaved away for three years at their project, only to have their eyes put out so that they couldn't repeat their engineering marvel for other patrons. In fact the pair received a generous pension – presumably too dull an outcome for the city's folklorists. The bell on the tower's roof terrace is struck by two bronze wild men known as "The Moors", because of their dark patina. Almost completely replaced in the 1750s, the clock's mechanism has been frequently overhauled since – most recently (and controversially) during a decade-long restoration of the whole tower, completed in 2006. You can take an hour-long guided tour of the interior, which stops on each of the five floors to explicate the history and the workings of this complex machine.

The Procuratie

MAP P.26, POCKET MAP G14–15
Away to the left of the Torre dell'Orologio stretches the **Procuratie Vecchie**, begun around 1500 to designs by Mauro Codussi, who also designed much of the clock tower. Once the home of

the **Procurators of San Marco**, whose responsibilities included the upkeep of the Basilica and the administration of the other government-owned properties, the block earned substantial rents for the city coffers: the upper floors housed some of the choicest apartments in town, while the ground floor was leased to shopkeepers and craftsmen, as is still the case.

Within a century or so, the procurators were moved across the Piazza to new premises, the **Procuratie Nuove**. When Napoleon's stepson, Eugène Beauharnais, was the Viceroy of Italy, he appropriated this building as a royal palace, and then discovered that the accommodation lacked a ballroom. He duly demolished the church of San Geminiano, which had filled part of the third side of the Piazza, and connected the Procuratie Nuove and Vecchie with a new wing, the **Ala Napoleonica**, containing the essential facility.

The Correr and archeological museums

MAP P.26, POCKET MAP G15
Ⓦ correr.visitmuve.it. Charge. Museums Pass or San Marco Museums Card.

Many of the rooms in the Ala Napoleonica and Procuratie Nuove are occupied by the **Museo Correr**, the chief civic museum of Venice, which is joined to the archeological museum and Sansovino's superb Libreria Sansoviniana.

Nobody could claim that the immense Correr collection is consistently fascinating, but it incorporates a picture gallery that more than makes up for the duller stretches, and its sections on Venetian society contain some eye-opening exhibits. You enter the Correr through the ballroom, where you'll see Canova's *Orpheus and Eurydice*, created when the sculptor was still in his teens. Then comes a suite of "Imperial rooms", which lead into a room in which you'll find Canova's *Venus Italica* and *Paris*: the pins in *Paris* were to enable Canova's assistants to map the coordinates onto the block of marble. Other pieces by Canova are on show in adjacent rooms, which you pass on your way out. After that you're into the historical collection, some of which will be enlightening only if you already have a pretty wide knowledge of Venetian history.

From here you pass directly into the Museo Archeologico, which is a somewhat scrappy museum, but look out for a head of Athena from the fourth century BC, a trio of wounded Gallic warriors (Roman copies of Hellenistic originals) and a phalanx of Roman emperors.

At the furthest point of the archeological museum a door opens into the hall of Sansovino's library (see page 32). Back in the Correr, a staircase beyond the sculpture section leads to the **Quadreria**, which may be no rival for the Accademia but nonetheless sets out clearly the evolution of painting in Venice from the thirteenth century to around 1500, and does contain some gems, including Jacopo de'Barbari's astonishing aerial view of Venice and a roomful of work by the Bellini family. The Correr's best-known possession, however, is the **Carpaccio** painting of two terminally bored women once known as *The Courtesans*, though in fact it depicts a couple of late fifteenth-century bourgeois ladies dressed in a style at which none of their contemporaries would have raised an eyebrow.

From the Quadreria you might be directed to the **Museo del Risorgimento**, which resumes the history of the city with its fall to Napoleon, then the itinerary passes through sections on Venetian festivals, crafts, trades and everyday life. Here the frivolous items are what catch the eye, especially a pair of eighteen-inch stacked shoes, as worn by the women in the Carpaccio painting.

The Piazzetta

MAP P.26, POCKET MAP G14–15

For much of the Republic's existence, the Piazzetta – the open space between the Basilica and the waterfront – was the area where the councillors of Venice would gather to scheme and curry favour. The

Libreria Sansoviniana

Coffee-drinking outside *Florian*

Piazzetta was also used for public executions: the usual site was the pavement between the two granite columns on the Molo, as this stretch of the waterfront is called. The last person to be executed here was one Domenico Storti, condemned to death in 1752 for the murder of his brother.

One of the columns is topped by a modern copy of a statue of **St Theodore**, the patron saint of Venice when it was dependent on Byzantium; the original (now in the Palazzo Ducale) was a compilation of a Roman torso, a head of Mithridates the Great, and miscellaneous bits and pieces carved in Venice in the fourteenth century (the dragon incorporates a crocodile, a torso and a head).

The **winged lion** on the other column is an ancient 3000kg bronze beast that was converted into a lion of St Mark by jamming a Bible under its paws. Its origins and provenance are unknown, and over the years scholars have argued fiercely and come to no reliable conclusion.

The Libreria Sansoviniana

MAP P.26, POCKET MAP G15
Ⓦ cultura.gov.it. Charge. Entrance via Museo Correr.

The Piazzetta is flanked by the Libreria Sansoviniana, also known as the Biblioteca Marciana. The impetus to build the library came from the bequest of Cardinal Bessarion, who left his celebrated hoard of classical texts to the Republic in 1468. Bessarion's books and manuscripts were first housed in San Marco and then in the Palazzo Ducale, but finally it was decided that a special building was needed. Jacopo Sansovino got the job, but the library wasn't finished until 1591, two decades after his death. Contemporaries regarded the Libreria as one of the supreme designs of the era, and the **main hall** is certainly one of the most beautiful rooms in the city: paintings by Veronese, Tintoretto, Andrea Schiavone and others cover the walls and ceiling.

The Zecca

MAP P.26, POCKET MAP G15
Attached to the Libreria, with its main facade to the lagoon, is Sansovino's first major building in Venice, the Zecca or Mint. Constructed in stone and iron to make it fireproof (most stonework in Venice is just skin-deep), it was built between 1537 and 1545 on the site occupied by the Mint since the thirteenth century. The rooms are now part of the library, but are not open to tourists.

The Giardinetti Reali

MAP P.26, POCKET MAP G15
Beyond the Zecca, and behind a barricade of postcard and toy gondola sellers, is a small public garden – the Giardinetti Reali – created by Eugène Beauharnais on the site of the state granaries and looking fabulous after a five-year restoration. It's the nearest place to the centre where you'll find a bench and the shade of a tree – and don't miss the wonderful Illy café in the Napoleonic pavilion.

Shops

Archimede Seguso

MAP P.26, POCKET MAP G14
Piazza San Marco 143
Ⓦ archimedeseguso.it.
Historic glassmaker, from a family who have been making glass since the fourteenth century. Famous for the glass vases created by the late Archimede Segusa inspired by his memory of the 1992 fire that destroyed La Fenice.

Martinuzzi

MAP P.26, POCKET MAP G15
Piazza San Marco 67a
Ⓦ martinuzzivenezia.com.
If cost is no object, call in at Martinuzzi, Venice's most durable and expensive purveyor of lace.

Salvadori Diamond Atelier

MAP P.26, POCKET MAP G15
Piazza San Marco 67 Ⓦ salvadori-venezia.com.
Purveyor of luxury watches and jewellery which dates back to the mid-nineteenth century.

Venini

MAP P.26, POCKET MAP G14
Piazzetta dei Leoncini 314 Ⓦ venini.com.
One of the more adventurous glass producers, Venini often employs designers from other fields of the applied arts.

Cafés and pasticcerie

Florian

MAP P.26, POCKET MAP G15
Piazza San Marco 56–59 Ⓦ caffeflorian.com.
The most famous café in Venice began life in 1720, when Florian Francesconi's *Venezia Trionfante* (Venice Triumphant) opened for business here, though the gorgeous interior – a frothy confection of mirrors, stucco and frescoes – is a nineteenth-century pastiche. Its prices match its pedigree: a simple cappuccino and pastry at an outside table will set you back a small fortune and you'll have to take out a small mortgage for a cocktail; if the "orchestra" is playing, a further surcharge is levied, as indeed it is at *Lavena* and *Quadri*. Probably the best value option is brunch, in essence the *Florian*'s take on an English afternoon tea, with a glass of prosecco and a hot drink. €€

Illy

MAP P.26, POCKET MAP G15
Giardini Reali Ⓦ illy.com.
Illy's flagship cafe, gleaming in the ruby glass of a contemporary chandelier, occupies a nineteenth-century pavilion on the edge of the Giardini Reali. Venetians reckon it serves the best coffee in the city. The miniature pastries, cakes and macarons are amazing, while in the evenings the focus switches to cocktails and spritzes. €

Lavena

MAP P.26, POCKET MAP G14
Piazza San Marco 133–134 Ⓦ caffelavena.it.
Wagner's favourite café (there's a commemorative plaque inside) is the second member of the Piazza's top-bracket trio. For privacy you can take a table in the narrow little gallery overlooking the bar. The coffee is in no way inferior to *Florian* or *Quadri*, and – unlike at *Florian* – you can keep down the price by drinking at the bar, though prices at the tables are no cheaper. €€

Quadri

MAP P.26, POCKET MAP G14
Piazza San Marco 120–124 Ⓦ alajmo.it.
Quadri can claim an even longer lineage than *Florian*, as coffee has been on sale here since the seventeenth century, and it's in the same price league too. It's not quite as pretty, and its name doesn't have quite the same lustre, possibly because Austrian officers patronized it during the occupation, while the natives stuck with *Florian*. €€

San Marco: north of the Piazza

From the Piazza the bulk of the pedestrian traffic flows north to the Rialto bridge along the Mercerie, the most browser-choked shopping mall in Venice. Only the churches of San Giuliano and San Salvador provide a diversion from the shops until you come to the Campo San Bartolomeo, the forecourt of the Rialto bridge and one of the locals' favoured spots for an after-work chat, along with the nearby Campo San Luca. Secreted in the folds of the alleyways hereabouts is the spiralling staircase called the Scala del Bovolo. And slotted away in a tiny square close to the Canal Grande you'll find the most delicate of Venice's museum buildings – the Palazzo Pésaro degli Orfei, home of the Museo Fortuny.

The Mercerie

MAP P.36, POCKET MAP F12–G14

The Mercerie, a chain of streets that starts under the Torre dell'Orologio and finishes at the Campo San Bartolomeo, is the most direct route between San Marco and the Rialto and has always been a prime site for Venice's shopkeepers – its mixture of slickness and tackiness ensnares more shoppers than any other part of Venice. (Each of the five links in the chain is a *merceria*: Merceria dell'Orologio, di San Zulian, del Capitello, di San Salvador and 2 Aprile.) Keep your eye open for one quirky feature: over the Sottoportego del Cappello (first left after the Torre) is a relief known as **La Vecia del Morter** – the Old Woman of the Mortar. The event it commemorates happened

Tourists shopping in Mercerie dell'Orologio

on the night of June 15, 1310, when the occupant of this house, an old woman named Giustina Rossi, looked out of her window and saw a contingent of Bajamonte Tiepolo's rebel army passing below. Possibly by accident, she knocked a stone mortar from her sill, and the missile landed on the skull of the standard-bearer, killing him outright. Seeing their flag go down, Tiepolo's troops panicked and fled.

San Giuliano

MAP P.36, POCKET MAP G13.
☎ 041 523538. Free.

The church of San Giuliano or San Zulian, at the San Marco end of the Mercerie, was rebuilt in the mid-sixteenth century with the generous aid of the physician Tommaso Rangone. His munificence is attested by the Greek and Hebrew inscriptions on the facade and by Alessandro Vittoria's portrait statue above the door.

San Salvador

MAP P.36, POCKET MAP F13.
☎ 041 523 6717. Free.

At its far end, the Mercerie veers right at the church of San Salvador or Salvatore, which was consecrated in 1177 by Pope Alexander III. The facade is less interesting than the interior, where, on the right-hand wall is Titian's *Annunciation* (1566), signed "*Fecit, fecit*" (Painted it, painted it) supposedly to emphasize the wonder of his continued creativity in extreme old age; a note on the rail in front of the picture records his death on August 25, 1576. Titian also painted the main altarpiece, a *Transfiguration*. The end of the right transept is filled by the **tomb** of Caterina Cornaro, one of the saddest figures in Venetian history. Born into one of Venice's pre-eminent families, she became Queen of Cyprus by marriage, and after her husband's death was forced to surrender the strategically crucial island to the doge. On

Carlo Goldoni, Campo San Bartolomeo

her return home she was led in triumph up the Canal Grande, as though her abdication had been voluntary, and then was presented with possession of the town of Ásolo as a token of gratitude. She died in 1510; this tomb was erected at the end of the century.

Campo San Bartolomeo

MAP P.36, POCKET MAP F12

A popular spot for Venetians to meet friends and window shop, Campo San Bartolomeo, terminus of the Mercerie, comes to life in the evenings; the handful of bars scattered about, adds to the atmosphere. The **church of San Bartolomeo** (free) has a landmark campanile, but its interior isn't thrilling: its organ panels, painted by Sebastiano del Piombo, are now housed in the Accademia, and its most famous picture, the altarpiece painted by Dürer at the request of the German merchant Christopher Fugger, long ago migrated to Prague.

Scala Contarini del Bovolo

Campo San Luca and Bacino Orseolo

MAP P.36, POCKET MAP F13–14

If the crush of San Bartolomeo is too much for you, you can retire to **Campo San Luca** (past the front of San Salvador and straight on), another open-air social centre, with some good bars and cafés. From Campo San Luca, Calle Goldoni is a direct route back to the Piazza, via the **Bacino Orseolo** – the city's major gondola depot, and one of the few places where you can admire the streamlining and balance of the boats without being hassled.

The Scala del Bovolo

MAP P.36, POCKET MAP E14
Campo Manin
ⓦ gioiellinascostidivenezia.it. Charge.

Campo Manin – where, unusually, the most conspicuous building is a modern one, Pier Luigi Nervi's Cassa di Risparmio di

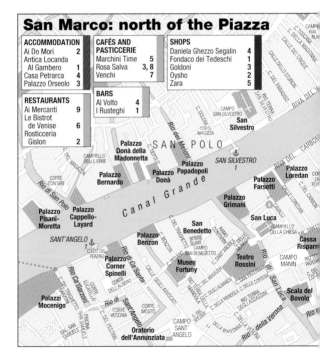

San Marco: north of the Piazza

ACCOMMODATION	
Ai Do Mori	2
Antica Locanda Al Gambero	1
Casa Petrarca	4
Palazzo Orseolo	3

CAFÉS AND PASTICCERIE	
Marchini Time	5
Rosa Salva	3, 8
Venchi	7

SHOPS	
Daniela Ghezzo Segalin	4
Fondaco dei Tedeschi	1
Goldoni	3
Oysho	2
Zara	5

RESTAURANTS	
Ai Mercanti	9
Le Bistrot de Venise	6
Rosticceria Gislon	2

BARS	
Al Volto	4
I Rusteghi	1

Venezia – was enlarged in 1871 to make room for the monument to Daniele Manin, the lawyer who was the leader of a revolt against the Austrians in 1848–49. On the wall of the alley on the south side of the campo, a sign directs you to the staircase known as the **Scala Contarini del Bovolo** (a *bovolo* is a snail shell in Venetian dialect). It was added to the Palazzo Contarini around 1500, perhaps to save space indoors while also making an impression on the neighbours. It's clever design makes it appear taller than it actually is, though the view of the staircase is perhaps more impressive than the view from it.

The Museo Fortuny

MAP P.36, POCKET MAP D14
Campo San Benedetto Ⓦ fortuny.visitmuve.it.
Charge. Maximum 75 visitors at a time.
The Museo Fortuny is close at hand, hidden away in a charming backwater campo you'd never accidentally pass. Born in Catalonia, **Mariano Fortuny** (1871–1949) is famous for inventing a still-secret technique for printing fabrics so lush and textured they looked like woven brocades, and for the body-clinging silk dresses so finely pleated that they could allegedly be threaded through a wedding ring. However, Fortuny was also a painter, architect, photographer, theatre designer and sculptor, and the contents of this rickety and atmospheric palazzo reflect his versatility. The highlight perhaps is the recently restored 'winter garden'– complete with 4-metre long sofa, abundant floor cushions and vases of pampas grass – a painted garden dripping with flowers and festooned with scantily clad nymphs. The top floor holds drawings, etchings, photographs and many of the tools used to create the famous fabrics.

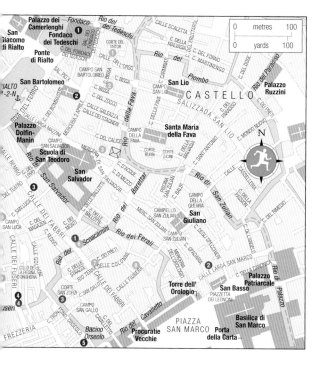

Shops

Daniela Ghezzo Segalin

MAP P.36, POCKET MAP F14
Calle dei Fuseri 4365 Ⓦ danielaghezzo.it.
Established in 1932 by Antonio
Segalin then run by his son
Rolando until 2003, this workshop
is now operated by Rolando's
star pupil Daniela Ghezzo, who
produces wonderful handmade
shoes, from sturdy brogues to
whimsical Carnival footwear. A
pair of Ghezzos can easily tip into
four figures.

Fondaco dei Tedeschi

MAP P.36, POCKET MAP F12
Ⓦ dfs.com.
When the Benetton Group bought
the Fondaco dei Tedeschi in 2008
and offered the city council a
six million euro sweetener for
the permission to develop it as a
shopping centre, the outrage was
understandably huge. The work
went ahead, however, to a project
designed by Dutch architect Rem
Koolhaas. Access to the luxury
shops – run by Duty Free giants
DFS – is free. If you want to go up
onto the panoramic roof terrace,
praised as a 'much-needed public
space' in *The Architectural Review*,
booking is obligatory, and although
free of charge, you are permitted to
stay for only fifteen minutes.

Goldoni

MAP P.36, POCKET MAP F13
Calle dei Fabbri 4742
Ⓦ veneziagoldoni.ubiklibri.it.
The best general bookshop in the
city; also keeps a good array of
maps and posters.

Oysho

MAP P.36, POCKET MAP F12
Campo S. Bartolomeo 5044–5182
Ⓦ oysho.com.
Inexpensive basics ranging from
underwear and pyjamas to puffa
jackets, fleeces and thermal
raincoats – ideal if Venice turns

out to be rainier or colder than
you anticipated.

Zara

MAP P.36, POCKET MAP F14
Calle S. Zorzi, 1176/A Ⓦ zara.com.
Possibly the world's most
gorgeously located branch of the
Spanish fashion chain – right on
the Bacino Orseolo – a reliable and
affordable first stop if you've been
surprised by the weather.

Cafés and pasticcerie

Marchini Time

MAP P.36, POCKET MAP E13
Campo San Luca 4589
Ⓦ facebook.com/pasticceriamarchini.
Sample the succulent *Marchini*
pastries with a cup of top-grade
coffee at this new, sleek café. €

Rosa Salva

MAP P.36, POCKET MAP F13 & G14
Merceria S. Salvador 5020 and Calle
Fiubera 950 Ⓦ rosasalva.it.
Decent coffee and pastries –
though the atmosphere can be a bit
brusque and businesslike. €

Venchi

MAP P.36, POCKET MAP F14
Calle dei Fabbri 998a Ⓦ venchi.com.
Founded in Turin in 1878, and
now with branches internationally
as well as in Italy *Venchi* creates
terrific chocolates and ice cream –
the hazelnut *gianduja* is a speciality.
There are also branches at Santa
Lucia station and on Ruga dei
Spezieri. €

Restaurants

Ai Mercanti

MAP P.36, POCKET MAP F14
Corte Coppo 4346 Ⓦ aimercanti.it.
This "*gastrosteria*" is one of the few
places in the San Marco *sestiere*
offering good-quality and creative

Venchi cioccolateria

cooking, with home-made bread, pasta and desserts. The menu has been simplified into just three courses – starters, mains and dessert – and there are several unique dishes (chicken with Greek yogurt, fennel, kumquat and olive crumble for example or baccalà with coconut and lemongrass). The dark wood and golden colour scheme is distinctive too. €€

Le Bistrot de Venise

MAP P.36, POCKET MAP F13
Calle dei Fabbri 4685
Ⓦ bistrotdevenise.com.
Though it looks a little like a French bistro, the menu here is based on the chef's research into historic Venetian recipes – such as gamberoni in saor (large prawns in agrodolce with a 'milk' of pine nuts) and spaghetti with cuttlefish ink topped with cuttlefish and saffron. There are several tasting menus if you want to push the boat out. €€€

Rosticceria Gislon

MAP P.36, POCKET MAP F12
Calle della Bissa 5424 Ⓣ 0415223569.
Downstairs it's a sort of glorified snack-bar, serving pizzas and set meals the trick is to first grab a place at the tables along

the windows, then order from the counter. Good if you need to refuel quickly and cheaply. There's a slightly less rudimentary restaurant upstairs, where prices are considerably higher for no great increase in quality. €

Bars

Al Volto

MAP P.36, POCKET MAP E13
Calle Cavalli 4081 Ⓦ enotecaalvolto.com.
This dark little bar founded in 1936 is an *enoteca* in the true sense of the word – 1300 wines from Italy and elsewhere, 100 of them served by the glass, some cheap, many not. It is a classic place for *ombra e cicheti*, a glass of wine and a few pre-prandial nibbles, spread out along the bar in traditional Venetian style.

I Rusteghi

MAP P.36, POCKET MAP F12
Corte del Tintor 5513 Ⓦ airusteghi.com.
Small *osteria*, secreted away in a tiny courtyard close to Campo San Bartolomeo. Great *cicheti*, nice wine, congenial host – plus a few outside tables. The perfect place for a quiet snack in the San Marco area.

San Marco: west of the Piazza

Leaving the Piazza by the west side you enter another major shopping district, where the clientele is drawn predominantly from Venice's well-heeled citizens or from the five-star tourists staying in the hotels that overlook the end of the Canal Grande. To a high proportion of visitors, this part of the city is principally the place to go for buying Gucci or Armani, or – for the less-consumer minded – the route to the Accademia, but there are things to see here apart from the latest creations from Milan and Paris – the extraordinary Baroque facades of Santa Maria del Giglio and San Moisè, for instance, or the graceful Santo Stefano, which rises at the end of one of the largest and most attractive squares in Venice.

San Moisè

MAP P.42, POCKET MAP F15
Campo San Moisè Ⓦ visitvenezia.eu.
San Moisè, which was founded in the eighth century, would be the runaway winner of any poll for the ugliest church in Venice. The church's name means "Saint Moses", the Venetians here

Basilica de San Moisè

following the Byzantine custom of canonizing Old Testament figures, while simultaneously honouring Moisè Venier, who paid for a rebuilding way back in the tenth century. Its facade, featuring a species of camel unknown to zoology, was sculpted largely by Heinrich Meyring in 1668 and was financed by the Fini family, whose portraits occupy prime positions. If you think this bloated display of fauna and flora is in questionable taste, wait till you see the miniature mountain he carved as the main altarpiece, representing *Mount Sinai with Moses Receiving the Tablets*.

Calle Larga XXII Marzo

MAP P.42, POCKET MAP E15–F15
If you're looking for a designer handbag, heirloom watch, or a new designer suit, then you'll probably find what you're after on or around the broad Calle Larga XXII Marzo, which begins over the canal from San Moisè. Many of the streets off the western side of the Piazza feature names such as Versace, Gucci, Ferragamo, Bulgari, Prada and Vuitton lurking around every corner.

Interior of La Fenice theatre

La Fenice

MAP P.42, POCKET MAP E15
Campo S. Fantin 1965 Ⓦ teatrolafenice.it.
Charge.

Halfway along Calle Larga XXII
Marzo, on the right, Calle del
Sartor da Veste takes you over
a canal and into **Campo San
Fantin**. The square is dominated
by the Teatro la Fenice, which
is the oldest and largest theatre
in Venice. Giannantonio Selva's
gaunt Neoclassical design was
not deemed a great success on its
inauguration on December 26,
1792, but nonetheless very little of
the exterior was changed when the
place had to be rebuilt after a fire
took place in 1836. Similarly, when
La Fenice was again destroyed by
fire on the night of January 29,
1996, it was decided to rebuild it as
a replica of Selva's theatre: after all,
its acoustics were superb and – with
a capacity of just nine hundred
people – it had an inspiringly
intimate atmosphere. La Fenice saw
some significant musical events in
the twentieth century – Stravinsky's
The Rake's Progress and Britten's
The Turn of the Screw were both
premiered here – but the music
scene was way more exciting in
the nineteenth century, when, in
addition to staging the premieres
of operas by Rossini, Bellini and
Verdi (*Rigoletto* and *La Traviata*
both opened here), it became the
focal point for a series of protests
against the occupying Austrian
army. The theatre is open during
the day for tours (audioguide or
app included in entry price). For
information on how to get tickets
for performances, see page 47.

Santa Maria del Giglio

MAP P.42, POCKET MAP E15
Campo Santa Maria del Giglio
Ⓦ visitvenezia.eu. Free.

Back on the route to the
Accademia, another extremely
odd church awaits – Santa Maria
del Giglio (Mary of the Lily),
commonly known as Santa Maria
Zobenigo, an alternative title
derived from the name of the
family who founded it in the ninth
century. The exterior features not
a single unequivocally Christian
image: the main statues are of
the five **Barbaro** brothers, who
financed the rebuilding of the
church in 1678; Virtue, Honour,
Fame and Wisdom hover at a
respectful distance; and relief

maps at eye level depict the towns distinguished with the brothers' presence in the course of their military and diplomatic careers. The interior, full to bursting with devotional pictures and sculptures, overcompensates for the impiety of the exterior.

San Maurizio and the Scuola degli Albanesi

MAP P.42, POCKET MAP D15

Campo San Maurizio

Ⓦ museodellamusica.com. Free.

The tilting campanile of **Santo Stefano** looms into view over the vapid and deconsecrated church of San Maurizio, which contains the Museo della Musica, a display of Baroque musical instruments spanning over three centuries, with a particularly fabulous collection of violins and other strings. A few metres away, at the head of Calle del Piovan, stands a diminutive building that was once the **Scuola**

degli Albanesi, the confraternity of the city's Albanian community; it was established in 1497 and the reliefs on the facade date from shortly after that.

Campo Santo Stefano

MAP P.42, POCKET MAP D15

The church of Santo Stefano closes one end of the spacious and lively Campo Santo Stefano, a good place to stop for a drink in one of its cafés. The campo has an alias – Campo Francesco Morosini – that comes from a former inhabitant of the **palazzo** at no. 2802. The last doge to serve as military commander of the Republic (1688–94), **Francesco Morosini** became a Venetian hero with his victories in the Peloponnese, but is notorious elsewhere as the man who lobbed a missile through the roof of the Parthenon, detonating the Turkish gunpowder barrels that had been stored there.

San Marco: west of the Piazza

Santo Stefano

MAP P.42, POCKET MAP D14–15
Campo Santo Stefano Ⓦ visitvenezia.eu. Free.
The church of Santo Stefano is
notable for its Gothic doorway and
beautiful **ship's keel roof**, both
of which date from the fifteenth
century, the last phase of the
church's construction. The airy and
calm interior is one of the most
pleasant places in Venice just to sit
and think, but it also contains some
major works of art, notably in the
picture-packed sacristy, where you'll
find a *St Lawrence* and a *St Nicholas
of Bari* by Bartolomeo Vivarini, a
Crucifix by Paolo Veneziano, and a
trio of late works by Tintoretto.

Campiello Nuovo

MAP P.42, POCKET MAP D14
Nearby Campiello Nuovo was
formerly the churchyard of Santo
Stefano, and was used as a burial
pit during the catastrophic plague
of 1630, which accounts for the

Statue of Niccolò Tommaseo, Santo Stefano

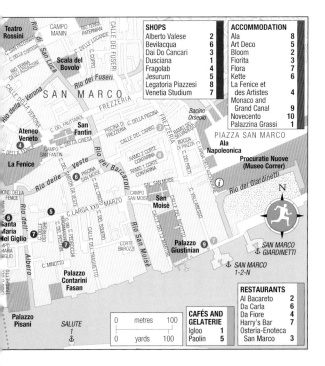

SHOPS

Alberto Valese	2
Bevilacqua	6
Dai Do Cancari	3
Dusciana	1
Fragolab	4
Jesurum	5
Legatoria Piazzesi	8
Venetia Studium	7

ACCOMMODATION

Ala	8
Art Deco	5
Bloom	2
Fiorita	3
Flora	7
Kette	6
La Fenice et des Artistes	4
Monaco and Grand Canal	9
Novecento	10
Palazzina Grassi	1

CAFÉS AND GELATERIE

Igloo	1
Paolin	5

RESTAURANTS

Al Bacareto	2
Da Carla	6
Da Fiore	4
Harry's Bar	7
Osteria-Enoteca San Marco	3

square's peculiar raised pavement. Such was the volume of corpses interred here that for health reasons the site remained closed to the public from then until 1838.

Campiello Pisani
MAP P.42, POCKET MAP E16
Campiello Pisani is a forecourt to the Palazzo Pisani, one of the biggest houses in the city, and now the Conservatory of Music. Work began on it in the early seventeenth century, continued for over a century, and was at last brought to a halt by the government, which decided that the Pisani, among the city's richest banking families, were getting ideas above their station. Had the Pisani got their way, they wouldn't have stopped building until they reached the Canal Grande.

San Samuele
MAP P.42, POCKET MAP C15
Campo San Samuele ⓦ savevenice.org.
From opposite the entrance to Santo Stefano church, Calle delle Botteghe and Crosera lead up to Salizzada San Samuele, a route that takes you past the house in which Paolo Veronese lived his final years, and on to **Campo San Samuele**. Built in the late twelfth century and not much altered since, the **campanile** of San Samuele is one of the oldest

in the city. The church itself was largely reconstructed in the late seventeenth century, though its frescoes, dating back to the fifteenth century, were restored in 2001 by Save Venice. Casanova began to train for the priesthood here, and aged 15 found love letters in the collection bowl after he had preached for the first time. He was chastised by the parish priest for wearing too much perfume and paying undue attention to the curling of his hair. When Casanova refused to comply, the priest crept into his bedroom while he was sleeping and "with sharp scissors pitilessly cut off all the hair at the front of my head, from one ear to the other."

Palazzo Grassi
MAP P.42, POCKET MAP C15
Campo San Samuele 3231 ⓦ palazzograssi.it.
Dwarfing San Samuele, the Palazzo Grassi became famous in the twenty years it was run by Fiat for its restoration by Gae Aulenti and flamboyantly blockbusting exhibitions on subjects such as the Celts, the Pharaohs and the Phoenicians. In 2005 it was acquired by the phenomenally wealthy François Pinault, who uses its exhibition space for contemporary art, often drawing on work from his own collection (see page 50).

The Palazzo Grassi

Shops

Alberto Valese

MAP P.42, POCKET MAP D14
Campo San Stefano 3471
Ⓦ albertovalese-ebru.it.

Valese not only produces the most luscious marbled papers in Venice, but also transfers the designs onto silk scarves and a variety of ornaments; he uses a Turkish marbling technique called *ebrû* (meaning cloudy) – hence the alternative name of his shop (Ebrû).

Bevilacqua

MAP P.42, POCKET MAP E15
Campo Santa Maria del Giglio 2520
Ⓦ bevilacquatessuti.com.

The Bevilacqua family has been weaving silk in Venice since around 1700, and the family company – established in 1875 – is famed throughout Italy for its patterned velvets, satins and other luxurious materials. Many of its fabrics are manufactured using eighteenth-century weaving techniques. Prices are eye-popping.

Dai Do Cancari

MAP P.42, POCKET MAP D14
Calle delle Botteghe 3455
Ⓦ daidocancari.it.

Perhaps Venice's best wine shop, selling scores of Italy's finest vintages. The range of eminently affordable draught wine (*vino sfuso*) from the Treviso area is well worth exploring – look out for reds made from the Veneto varietal Refosco, and local whites such as Tokai, Verduzzo Dorato and Prosecco Tranquillo.

Dusciana

MAP P.42, POCKET MAP C14
Calle de le Carrozze, San Marco 3283
Ⓦ dusciana.com.

Former mosaic artist who seeks colour and abstract patterns in the natural world, plays with them to create original prints and fabulous costume jewellery. Fabulous bags, scarves, kimonos and trousers – even medals – at extremely fair prices.

Fragolab

MAP P.42, POCKET MAP D15
Calle delle Botteghe 2968
Ⓦ fragolabo.com.

Hand-made clothes – designed to fit anyone – in classic, rather sculptural, shapes in quality wools, velvets, cord and linen designed and made by Franca Goppion. She also creates striking jewellery, each a miniature work of art. Prices surprisingly low.

Jesurum

MAP P.42, POCKET MAP E15
Calle del Sartor da Veste 2024
Ⓦ jesurum.it.

Founded by Michelangelo, Jesurum rocked the lace world with polychrome creations way back in 1878, rapidly becoming known for its exquisite and innovative lace. These days the focus is on luxurious bed, bath and table linens fusing contemporary design with traditional techniques.

Legatoria Piazzesi

MAP P.42, POCKET MAP D15
Campiello della Feltrina 2511
Ⓣ 348 144 5367.

Located near Santa Maria del Giglio, this paper-producer was founded in 1851 and claims to be the oldest such shop in Italy. Using the wooden-block method of printing, it makes stunning hand-printed papers, cards and pocket diaries.

Venetia Studium

MAP P.42, POCKET MAP E15 Ⓦ delphos.com.
Calle delle Ostreghe 2425

Genuine Fortuny creations cost a fortune, but this place sells well-priced Fortuny-approved replicas of lamps, bags and scarves. There are other Venice branches, the biggest of which is in Dorsoduro, at Calle del Bastion 186, between the Guggenheim and the Salute.

Inside Alberto Valese

Cafés and gelaterie

Igloo

MAP P.42, POCKET MAP E14
Calle della Mandola 3651 ☎ 041 528 9185.
Luscious home-made ice cream to take away – the summer fruit concoctions are especially delicious. €

Paolin

MAP P.42, POCKET MAP D15
Campo S. Stefano 2962 ☎ 041 522 5576.
Campo Santo Stefano has a seemingly ever-increasing number of cafés and restaurants, but *Paolin*, founded in 1760, has been here longer than any of them. In addition to drinks it serves some of the best ice cream in Venice, and the outside tables have a very nice setting. €

Restaurants

Al Bacareto

MAP P.42, POCKET MAP C14
San Samuele 3447 ⓦ bacareto.it
Tucked away on the north side of Santo Stefano, *Al Bacareto* has been in business here for more than forty years and remains one of the most genuine and welcoming places in Venice's San Marco *sestiere*. In recent years it has been getting smarter and more expensive, but it's still good value, and if you're watching the pennies you can always eat at the bar, where the *cicheti* are outstanding. In the summer there is also seating outside. €€€

Da Carla

MAP P.42, POCKET MAP F15
Sottoportego Corte Contarina 1535a
ⓦ osteriadacarla.it.
Hidden down a *sottoportego* off the west side of Frezzeria, *Da Carla* has a battered old sign that's rather misleading, as this place has been refashioned as a slick modern *osteria*. The menu is short but the food is well prepared, and the prices (pasta dishes around €10, main courses under €20) make this one of the best places for a simple meal close to the Piazza. The service – polite and attentive – is better than average for this part of town. €€

Da Fiore

MAP P.42, POCKET MAP D14
Calle delle Botteghe 3461 ⓦ dafiore.it.
This popular bacaro-trattoria is a very good choice indeed for typical Venetian cuisine. The nice small bar (*bacaro*) offers good *cicheti* plus a small menu of daily specials at far lower prices than in the restaurant. €€

Harry's Bar

MAP P.42, POCKET MAP F15
Calle Vallaresso 1323 ⓦ cipriani.com.
Harry's Bar is perhaps not only the most famous of Venice's bars, but the most famous bar in the world. The Bellini – one third fresh white peach juice to two-thirds prosecco was invented here, as was *carpaccio* – translucent-thin slices of raw beef – but neither the food nor the drink embody

what makes *Harry's* unique. Jan Morris described the atmosphere as 'striking and pungent' and somehow, whoever the clientele of the moment might be – Venetian aristocrats or hen-nighters from Huddersfield – *Harry's* (or rather its bar staff) remain unruffled. *Harry's* was founded in 1931 by Giuseppe Cipriani, who named it after Harry Pickering, a young American who, by way of thanks for a loan that Cipriani had earlier given him to see him through a crisis, loaned Cipriani enough cash to set up his own bar. The Cipriani family continued to run the place until 2013, when, saddled with debts of several million euros, they were forced to cede control to an investment fund. €€€€

Osteria-Enoteca San Marco

MAP P.42, POCKET MAP F14
Frezzeria 1610 ⓦ osteriasanmarco.it.
As you'd expect for a place so close to the Piazza, this classy modern *osteria* is far from cheap, but the prices are not madly unreasonable for the quality of the food and location – and the wine list is very

Da Carla

good. Classical mouth-watering antipasti (scallops with pea puree, cabbage and bacon, or beef tartare with asparagus and cured egg yolk) and home-made pasta. Between lunchtime and dinner you can sip wine at the bar. €€€

Opera

La Fenice

MAP P.42, POCKET MAP E15
Campo San Fantin ⓦ teatrolafenice.it.
The third-ranking Italian opera house after Milan's La Scala and Naples' San Carlo, La Fenice has opera and ballet performances throughout the year; classical concerts are held in the Fenice's Sale Apollinee. Seats for the opera cost around €65–170 on most nights, but you'll pay rather more for the opening night of a production; prices are a little lower mid-week than at the weekend, and restricted-view seats are sometimes available for very little indeed. Tickets can be bought online, at the Fenice box office and at several other points scattered about the city and listed on the website.

Dorsoduro

There weren't many places among the lagoon's mudbanks where Venice's early settlers could be confident that their dwellings wouldn't slither down into the water, but with Dorsoduro they were on relatively solid ground, it being the largest area of firm silt in the city's centre, hence the name, which means 'hard back'. The main draw here is the Gallerie dell'Accademia, the city's top art gallery, while the most conspicuous building is the huge Baroque church of Santa Maria della Salute right on the water. More notable for art, San Sebastiano was the parish church of Paolo Veronese, while Giambattista Tiepolo is represented at the Scuola Grande dei Carmini. Modern art is also in evidence – at the small yet impressive Guggenheim Collection and at the Punta della Dogana, home to the vast art collection of François Pinault.

The Accademia

MAP P.50, POCKET MAP C16
Calle della Carità 1050
ⓦ gallerieaccademia.it. Charge.

The **Accademia** is one of Venice's main tourist sights; admission is restricted to three hundred people at a time. The most important works are displayed on the upper floor, while the new lower galleries (formerly occupied by the art school) show works until recently confined to storage. Begin your visit upstairs.

The first room is filled with pieces by the earliest-known individual Venetian painters, Paolo Veneziano and his follower Lorenzo Veneziano. Next come large altarpieces from the late fifteenth and early sixteenth centuries, including works by Giovanni Bellini, Cima da Conegliano and Vittore Carpaccio.

Carpaccio's strange *Crucifixion and Glorification of the Ten Thousand Martyrs of Mount Ararat* is the room's most gruesome painting, and the most charming is by him too: *The Presentation of Jesus in the Temple*, with its wingless, lute-playing angel.

As you continue, the characteristically soft and rich Venetian palette begins to emerge. Outstanding are a series of *Madonnas* and a *Pietà* by **Giovanni Bellini**, and two pieces by **Giorgione** – his *Portrait of an Old Woman* and the so-called *Tempest* (c.1500).

Next come Tintoretto, Titian and Veronese, while in vast room 10, one whole wall is needed for *Christ in the House of Levi* by **Paolo Veronese**. Originally called *The Last Supper*, this picture brought down on Veronese the wrath of the

Dorsoduro Museum Mile

The museums of Dorsoduro – The Accademia, the Guggenheim, Punta della Dogana and Palazzo Cini – have formed a consortium which means that if you visit one of the museums you are entitled to a discount at the others for seven days.

Inquisition; Inquisitors objected to the inclusion of "buffoons, drunkards, Germans, dwarfs, and similar indecencies" in the sacred scene. Veronese's insouciant response was simply to change the title. Among **Tintoretto**'s works is the painting that made his reputation: *St Mark Freeing a Slave* (1548), showing St Mark's intervention at the execution of a slave who had defied his master by travelling to the Evangelist's shrine. Opposite is **Titian**'s *Pietà* (1576), painted for his own tomb in the Frari and completed after his death by Palma il Giovane.

After a large hall that houses numerous paintings by two of Venice's most significant artistic dynasties, the **Vivarini** and **Bellini** families, you come to room 20, which is entirely filled by the cycle *The Miracles of the Relic of the Cross*. Produced by various artists (most notably Gentile Bellini) between 1494 and 1501, it was commissioned by the Scuola Grande di San Giovanni Evangelista.

Another remarkable cycle fills room 21 – **Carpaccio**'s *Story of St Ursula*, painted for the Scuola di Sant'Orsola at San Zanipolo in 1490–94. A superlative exercise in pictorial narrative, the paintings are a record of Venice's domestic architecture and costume at the close of the fifteenth century. After this, you leave the Accademia through a door beneath **Titian**'s *Presentation of the Virgin* (1539), still occupying the space for which it was painted.

Nothing in the ground-floor galleries matches the impact of the upper rooms, but there are some fine pieces, including Giambattista Tiepolo's virtuoso *St Helena Discovering the Cross*. **Canaletto** and **Guardi** are also here, along with quasi-documentary interiors by **Pietro Longhi**, and a large quantity of sculptures and reliefs by the great Neoclassical sculptor **Antonio**

View of The Guggenheim

Canova. Also on show are a series of portraits by **Rosalba Carriera**, one of the very few women in the Accademia's collection. Carriera's work established the use of pastel as a medium in its own right, rather than as a preparation for oil paint – her moving *Self-Portrait*, done at a time when her eyesight was beginning to fail, is a high point.

The Guggenheim

MAP P.50, POCKET MAP D16
Calle San Cristofero 701 Ⓦ guggenheim-venice.it. Charge.

Until François Pinault came to town, the city's most famous showing of modern art was the **Peggy Guggenheim Collection**, which is installed in the quarter-built **Palazzo Venier dei Leoni**, a bit farther up the Canal Grande from the Accademia.

In the early years of the twentieth century the leading lights of the Futurist movement came here for the parties thrown by the dotty Marchesa Casati, who was fond of stunts like setting wild cats and apes loose in the palazzo garden, among plants sprayed lilac for the occasion. Peggy Guggenheim, a considerably more discerning patron of the arts, moved into the palace in 1949; since her death in 1979 the Guggenheim Foundation has administered the place, and has turned her private collection into one of the city's glossiest museums – and the second most popular after the Accademia. It's a small but generally top-quality assembly of twentieth-century art and a prime venue for touring exhibitions. In the permanent collection the core pieces include Brancusi's *Bird in Space* and *Maestra*, De Chirico's *Red Tower* and *Nostalgia of the Poet*, Max Ernst's *Robing of the Bride* (Guggenheim was married to Ernst in the 1940s), sculpture by Laurens and Lipchitz, and works by Malevich and Schwitters; other artists include Picasso, Braque, Chagall, Pollock, Duchamp, Giacometti, Picabia and Magritte. Paintings from the 2012 Schulhof bequest focus on the post-war

journey of abstraction –with stand-out canvasses by Antoni Tapies, Mark Rothko, Cy Twombly and Hans Hoffman. Marino Marini's *Angel of the Citadel*, out on the terrace, flaunts his erection at the passing canal traffic; more decorous pieces by Giacometti, Moore, Paolozzi and others are planted in the garden, surrounding Peggy Guggenheim's burial place.

The Punta della Dogana

MAP P.50, POCKET MAP F16
Fondamenta Salute Ⓦ palazzograssi.it.
Charge.

The Punta della Dogana occupies the Dogana di Mare, the city's old customs house, a striking one-storey triangular building which lies in the shadow of the Salute church at the tip of the Canal Grande. In 2009 it was converted by Japanese architect Tadao Ando into a showcase for the colossal art collection of François Pinault, the

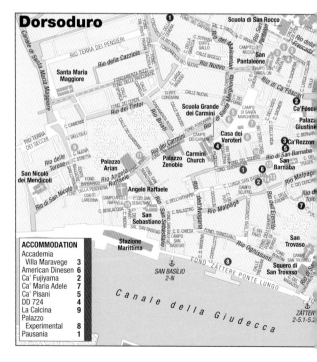

ACCOMMODATION
Accademia
   Villa Maravege   3
American Dinesen   6
Ca' Fujiyama   2
Ca' Maria Adele   7
Ca' Pisani   5
DD 724   4
La Calcina   9
Palazzo
   Experimental   8
Pausania   1

co-owner of Palazzo Grassi (see page 44). Hundreds of works are on display at any one time, and as Pinault has invested in most of the really big names of the current art scene, you can expect to see pieces by the likes of Cindy Sherman, Luc Tuymans, Cy Twombly, Thomas Schütte, Maurizio Cattelan, Jeff Koons, the Chapman brothers and Marlene Dumas.

Santa Maria della Salute

MAP P.50, POCKET MAP E16
Fondamenta Salute Ⓦ visitvenezia.eu. Free.
In 1630–31 Venice was devastated by a plague that exterminated nearly 95,000 of the lagoon's population – one person in three. In October 1630 the Senate decreed that a new church would be dedicated to Mary if the city were saved, and the result was Santa Maria della Salute (*salute* meaning "health" and "salvation"). Resting on a platform of more than

Inside the Punta della Dogana

one hundred thousand wooden piles, the Salute took half a century to build; its architect, **Baldassare Longhena**, was only 26 years old

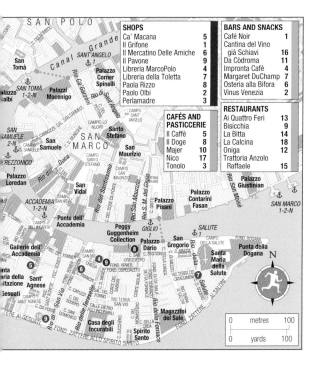

SHOPS	
Ca' Macana	5
Il Grifone	1
Il Mercatino Delle Amiche	6
Il Pavone	9
Libreria MarcoPolo	4
Libreria della Toletta	7
Paola Rizzo	8
Paolo Olbi	2
Perlamadre	3

CAFÉS AND PASTICCERIE	
Il Caffè	5
Il Doge	8
Majer	10
Nico	17
Tonolo	3

BARS AND SNACKS	
Café Noir	1
Cantina del Vino già Schiavi	16
Da Còdroma	11
Impronta Cafè	4
Margaret DuChamp	7
Osteria alla Bifora	6
Vinus Venezia	2

RESTAURANTS	
Ai Quattro Feri	13
Bisicchia	9
La Bitta	14
La Calcina	18
Oniga	12
Trattoria Anzolo Raffaele	15

when his proposal was accepted and lived just long enough to see it finished, in 1681.

Each year on November 21 (the feast of the Presentation of the Virgin) the Signoria is processed from San Marco to the Salute for a service of thanksgiving, crossing the Canal Grande on a pontoon bridge laid from Santa Maria del Giglio. The Festa della Madonna della Salute is still a major event in the Venetian calendar.

The form of the Salute is replete with Marian symbolism: the octagonal plan and eight facades allude to the eight-pointed Marian star, for example, while the huge dome represents Mary's crown and the centralized plan is a conventional symbol of the Virgin's womb. Less arcane symbolism is at work on the **high altar**, where the Virgin and Child rescue Venice (kneeling woman) from the plague (old woman); in attendance are saints Mark and Lorenzo Giustiniani, first Patriarch of Venice.

The most notable paintings in the Salute are the **Titian** pieces brought from the suppressed church of Santo Spirito in Isola in 1656, and now displayed in the sacristy (€3). Tintoretto has included himself in the dramatis personae of his *Marriage at Cana* (1561) – he's the first Apostle on the left.

The Záttere

MAP P.50, POCKET MAP C7–G7

Known collectively as the **Záttere**, the sequence of waterfront pavements between the Punta della Dogana and the Stazione Maríttima are now a popular place for a stroll or a waterside meal, but were formerly the place where most of the bulky goods coming into Venice were unloaded onto floating rafts called *záttere*.

The Gesuati

MAP P.50, POCKET MAP E8
Fondamenta delle Zattere
Ⓦ chorusvenezia.org. Charge.

As you walk along the Záttere from the mouth of the Canal

Gondolas

The earliest mention of a gondola is in a decree of 1094, but the vessel of that period bore little resemblance to today's streamlined thoroughbred. As late as the thirteenth century the gondola was a twelve-oared beast with an iron beak – an adornment that evolved into the saw-toothed projection called the **ferro**, which fronts the modern gondola. Over the next two centuries the gondola shrank to something near its present dimensions, developed multicoloured coverings and sprouted the little chair on carved legs that it still carries. The gondola's distinctive oarlock, an elaborately convoluted lump of walnut or cherry wood known as a **forcola**, which permits the long oar to be used in eight different positions, reached something like its present form at this time too.

There's been little alteration in the gondola's dimensions and construction since the end of the seventeenth century: the only significant changes have been adjustments of the gondola's asymmetric line to compensate for the weight of the gondolier. All gondolas are 10.87m long and 1.42m wide at their broadest point, and are assembled from nearly three hundred pieces of seasoned mahogany, elm, oak, lime, walnut, fir, cherry and larch. Gondolas are regularly brought into the boatyards for repair, but each *squero* turns out only about four new gondolas a year.

Grande, the first building to break your stride for is the church of the **Gesuati** or Santa Maria del Rosario. Rebuilt in 1726–43, about fifty years after the church was taken over from the order of the Gesuati by the Dominicans, this was the first church designed by **Giorgio Massari**, an architect who often worked with **Giambattista Tiepolo**. Tiepolo painted the first altarpiece on the right, *The Virgin with SS. Catherine of Siena, Rose and Agnes* (c.1740), and the three magnificent ceiling panels, *Scenes from the Life of St Dominic* (1737–39), which are seen to best effect in the afternoon. The third altar on this side of the church is adorned with the painting *SS. Vincent Ferrer, Giacinto and Luigi Beltran* by Tiepolo's principal forerunner, Giambattista Piazzetta; opposite, the first altar has Sebastiano Ricci's *Pius V with SS. Thomas Aquinas and Peter Martyr* (1739), completing the church's array of Rococo propaganda on behalf of the exalted figures of Dominican orthodoxy, followed by a tragically intense *Crucifixion* by Tintoretto (c.1555) on the third altar.

San Trovaso

MAP P.50, POCKET MAP B16
Campo San Trovaso ☎ 041 522 2133.
Don't bother consulting your dictionary of saints for the dedicatee of **San Trovaso** church – the name's a baffling dialect version of Santi Gervasio e Protasio. Since its tenth-century foundation the church has had a chequered history, falling down once, and twice being destroyed by fire; this is the fourth incarnation, built from 1584 to 1657.

Venetian folklore has it that this church was the only neutral ground between the Nicolotti and the Castellani, the two factions into which the working-class citizens of the city were divided – the former, coming from the west and north of the city, were named after the

The Gesuati, or Santa Maria del Rosario

church of San Nicolò dei Mendicoli (see page 55), the latter, from the *sestieri* of Dorsoduro, San Marco and Castello, took their name from San Pietro di Castello. The rivals celebrated inter-marriages and other services here, but are said to have entered and departed by separate doors.

Inside, San Trovaso is spacious and somewhat characterless, but it does boast a pair of fine paintings by **Tintoretto**: *The Temptation of St Anthony*, in the chapel to the left of the high altar, and *The Last Supper* in the chapel at ninety degrees to it.

Squero di San Trovaso

MAP P.50, POCKET MAP B16/D8
Rio San Trovaso ⓦ squerosantrovaso.com.
Ten thousand gondolas operated on the canals of sixteenth-century Venice, when they were the standard form of transport to get around the city; nowadays the tourist trade is pretty well all that sustains the city's fleet of around five hundred boats, which provide steady employment for a couple of **squeri**, as the gondola yards are called. A display in the Museo Storico Navale (see page 96) takes you through the

construction of a gondola, but no abstract demonstration can equal the fascination of a working yard, and the most public one in Venice is the *squero* di San Trovaso, on the Záttere side of San Trovaso church. The San Trovaso *squero* was established in the seventeenth century and looks rather like an alpine farmhouse, a reflection of the architecture of the Dolomite villages from which many of Venice's gondola-builders once came.

San Sebastiano

MAP P.50, POCKET MAP C7
Campazzo San Sebastiano
ⓦ chorusvenezia.org. Charge.

At the end of the Záttere the barred gates of the Stazione Maríttima deflect you away from the waterfront and towards the church of San Sebastiano. The parish church of **Paolo Veronese**, it contains a group of resplendent paintings by him that gives it a place in his career comparable to that of San Rocco in the career of Tintoretto, but the church attracts nothing like the number of visitors that San Rocco gets.

Campazzo San Sebastiano

Veronese was still in his twenties when, thanks largely to his contacts with the Verona-born prior of San Samuele, he was asked to paint the ceiling of the **sacristy** with a *Coronation of the Virgin* and the *Four Evangelists* (1555); once that commission had been carried out, he decorated the **nave ceiling** with *Scenes from the Life of St Esther*. His next project, the dome of the chancel, was later destroyed, but the sequence he and his brother Benedetto then painted on the walls of the church and the nun's choir at the end of the 1550s has survived in pretty good shape. In the following decade he executed the last of the pictures, those on the **organ shutters** and around the **high altar** – on the left, *St Sebastian Leads SS Mark and Marcellian to Martyrdom*, and on the right, *The Second Martyrdom of St Sebastian*. Other riches include a late **Titian**, *St Nicholas* (on the left wall of the first chapel on the right), and the early sixteenth-century majolica pavement in the Cappello Lando, to the left of the chancel – in front of which is Veronese's tomb slab.

Angelo Raffaele

MAP P.50, POCKET MAP B7
Campo San Sebastiano
Ⓦ anzolomendicoli.it. Free.

On the far side of Campo San Sebastiano, the seventeenth-century church of **Angelo Raffaele** inspired Salley Vickers' evocative Venetian-set novel *Miss Garnett's Angel*. Inside, the organ loft above the entrance on the canal side is decorated with *Scenes from the Life of St Tobias*, painted by one or other of the **Guardi** brothers (nobody's sure which). Although small in scale, the free brushwork and imaginative composition make the panels among the most charming examples of Venetian Rococo, a fascinating counterpoint to the grander visions of Giambattista Tiepolo, the Guardis' brother-in-law.

San Nicolò dei Mendicoli

MAP P.50, POCKET MAP B7
Campo San Nicolò dei Mendicoli
Ⓦ anzolomendicoli.it.

Although it's located on the edge of the city, the church of **San Nicolò dei Mendicoli** is one of Venice's oldest, said to have been founded in the seventh century. Its long history is reflected in the fact that it gave its name to the **Nicolotti** faction (see page 53), whose titular head, the so-called *Gastaldo* or the *Doge dei Nicolotti*, was elected by the parishioners and then honoured by a ceremonial greeting from the Republic's doge.

The church has been rebuilt and altered at various times, and was last restored in the 1970s, when Nic Roeg used it as a setting for his movie *Don't Look Now*. In essence, however, its shape is still that of the Veneto-Byzantine structure raised here in the twelfth century, the date of its rugged campanile. The other conspicuous feature of the exterior is the fifteenth-century porch, a type of construction once common in Venice, and often used here as makeshift accommodation

for penurious nuns. The **interior** is a miscellany of periods and styles. Parts of the apse and the columns of the nave go back to the twelfth century, but the darkened gilded woodwork that gives the interior its rather overcast appearance was installed late in the sixteenth century, as were most of the paintings, many of which were painted by Alvise dal Friso and other pupils of Paolo Veronese.

Campo di Santa Margherita

MAP P.50, POCKET MAP A14

Campo di Santa Margherita is the social heart of Dorsoduro, and is one of the most appealing squares in the whole city. The Piazza San Marco nowadays is overrun with tourists, but Campo di Santa Margherita – the largest square on this side of the Canal Grande – belongs to the Venetians and retains a spirit of authenticity. Ringed by houses that date back as far as the fourteenth century, it's spacious and at the same time modest, taking its tone not from any grandiose architecture (it's one of very few squares with no *palazzo*), but from its cluster of market stalls and its plethora of bars and cafés, which draw a lot of their custom from the nearby university.

San Pantaleone

MAP P.50, POCKET MAP A13–14
Campo San Pantalon Ⓦ sanpantalon.it.

The church of San Pantaleone, to the north of Campo di Santa Margherita, has the most melodramatic **ceiling** in Venice. Painted on sixty panels, some of which jut out over the nave, *The Martyrdom and Apotheosis of St Pantaleone* kept **Gian Antonio Fumiani** busy from 1680 to 1704. Sadly, he never got the chance to bask in the glory of his labours – he died in a fall from the scaffolding from which he'd been working. In addition, the church possesses a fine picture by Antonio Vivarini

Santa Maria dei Carmini church tower

The core of this complex is now effectively a showcase for the art of **Giambattista Tiepolo**, who in the 1740s painted the wonderful ceiling of the upstairs hall.

The adjacent **Carmini** church, or Santa Maria del Carmelo, is a collage of architectural styles, with a sixteenth-century facade, a Gothic side doorway which preserves several Byzantine fragments, and a fourteenth-century basilican interior. A dull series of Baroque paintings illustrating the history of the Carmelite order covers a lot of space inside, but the second altar on the right has a *Nativity* by Cima da Conegliano (before 1510), and Lorenzo Lotto's *SS. Nicholas of Bari, John the Baptist and Lucy* (1529) – featuring what Bernard Berenson ranked as one of the most beautiful landscapes in all Italian art – hangs on the opposite side of the nave.

The Ponte dei Pugni
MAP P.50, POCKET MAP A15

Cutting down the side of the Carmini church takes you over the Rio di San Barnaba, along which a *fondamenta* runs to the church of San Barnaba. Just before the end of the *fondamenta* you pass the Ponte dei Pugni, one of several bridges with this name. Originally built without parapets, they were the sites of ritual battles between the Castellani and Nicolotti; this one is inset with marble footprints marking the starting positions. These massed brawls took place between September and Christmas, and obeyed a well-defined etiquette, with prescribed ways of issuing challenges and deploying the antagonists prior to the outbreak of hostilities, the aim of which was to gain possession of the bridge. The fights themselves, however, were sheer bedlam, and fatalities were commonplace, as the armies slugged it out with bare knuckles and steel-tipped lances made from hardened rushes. The

and Giovanni d'Alemagna (in the chapel to the left of the chancel) and Veronese's last painting, *St Pantaleone Healing a Boy* (second chapel on right).

The Carmini scuola and church
MAP P.50, POCKET MAP C6
Campo dei Carmini Ⓦ scuolagrandecarmini. it. Scuola charge, church free.

Just off Campo di Santa Margherita's southwest tip is the **Scuola Grande dei Carmini**, once the Venetian base of the Carmelites. Originating in Palestine towards the close of the twelfth century, the Carmelites blossomed during the Counter-Reformation, when they became the shock-troops through whom the cult of the Virgin could be disseminated. The Venetian Carmelites became immensely wealthy, and in the 1660s they called in an architect – probably Longhena – to re-design the property they had acquired.

lethal weaponry was outlawed in 1574, after a particularly bloody engagement that was arranged for the visit of Henry III of France, and in 1705 the punch-ups were finally banned, and less dangerous forms of competition, such as regattas, were encouraged instead.

San Barnaba

MAP P.50, POCKET MAP B15
Campo San Barnaba
Ⓦ leonardoavenezia.com. Charge.

The huge, damp-ridden San Barnaba church, built in 1749, with a trompe l'oeil ceiling painting of *St Barnabas in Glory* by Constantino Cedini, a follower of Tiepolo, has become home to an exhibition of replicas of the "machines of Leonardo".

Ca' Rezzonico

MAP P.50, POCKET MAP B15
Fondamenta Rezzonico
Ⓦ carezzonico.visitmuve.it. Charge.

The **Museo del Settecento Veneziano** – The Museum of the Venetian Eighteenth Century – spreads through most of the enormous Ca' Rezzonico, a palazzo that the city authorities bought in 1934 specifically as a home for the museum. It's never been one of the most popular of Venice's museums, but hopefully the major renovation, completed in 2023, will go some way to rectifying its unjustified neglect.

A man in constant demand in the early part of the eighteenth century was the Belluno sculptor-cum-woodcarver **Andrea Brustolon**, much of whose output consisted of wildly elaborate pieces of furniture, exemplified by the stuff on show in the Brustolon Room. The less fervid imaginations of **Giambattista Tiepolo** and his son **Giandomenico** are introduced in room 2 with the ceiling fresco celebrating Ludovico Rezzonico's marriage into the hugely powerful Savorgnan family in 1758. Beyond room 4, with its array of pastels

by **Rosalba Carriera**, you come to two other Tiepolo ceilings, enlivening the rooms overlooking the Canal Grande on each side of the main portego – an *Allegory of Merit* by Giambattista and Giandomenico, and *Nobility and Virtue Triumphing over Perfidy*, a solo effort by the father.

In the portego of the second floor hang the only two canal views by **Canaletto** on show in public galleries in Venice. The next suite of rooms contains the museum's most engaging paintings – Giandomenico Tiepolo's sequence of **frescoes from the Villa Zianigo** near Mestre, the Tiepolo family home. Begun in 1759, the frescoes were completed towards the end of the century, by which time Giandomenico's style was going out of fashion. There's an air of wistful melancholy in pictures such as *The New World* (1791), which shows a crowd turned out in its best attire at a Sunday fair. The following rooms display delightful portraits and depictions of everyday Venetian life by **Francesco Guardi** (including high-society recreation in the parlour of San Zaccaria's convent) and **Pietro Longhi**, whose artlessly candid work – such as a version of the famous *Rhinoceros* – has more than enough curiosity value to make up for its shortcomings in execution.

The low-ceilinged rooms of the third and fourth floor contain the Pinacoteca Egidio Martini, a large but rarely thrilling private donation of Venetian art from the fifteenth to twentieth centuries, but you do get a tremendous view across the rooftops from here, and there's one unusual exhibit: an old **pharmacy**, comprising a sequence of wood-panelled rooms heavily stocked with ceramic jars and glass bottles. Back on the ground floor, steps lead up to the Mestrovich collection, which is smaller and even less engrossing than the Martini bequest.

Shops

Ca' Macana

MAP P.50, POCKET MAP B15
Calle delle Botteghe 3215 Ⓦ camacana.com.
Terrific mask shop-cum-studio,
with perhaps the biggest stock in
the city; they also run mask-making
workshops and courses for adults
or children.

Il Grifone

MAP P.50, POCKET MAP C5
Fondamenta del Gaffaro 3516
Ⓦ ilgrifonevenezia.it.
Handmade briefcases, satchels,
purses, belts and other pieces
made from beautifully soft leather.
Reasonable prices.

Il Mercatino Delle Amiche

MAP P.50, POCKET MAP A15
Calle Lunga San Barnaba 2751
☎ 338 816 8240.
Vintage and pre-loved women's
clothes, usually with a fine collection
of classic jackets, coats and dresses.

Il Pavone

MAP P.50, POCKET MAP D16
Fondamenta Venier 721
Ⓦ ilpavonevenezia.com.
Nice wooden-block printed papers,
folders and so on, plus an interesting
line in personalized rubber stamps
and *Ex Libris* bookplates.

Libreria MarcoPolo

MAP P.50, POCKET MAP C6
Campo Santa Margherita 2899
Ⓦ libreriamarcopolo.com.
This fine independent bookshop,
run by an expat New Yorker, has
two branches – both on Campo
Santa Margherita, one mainly
for new titles, and the other with
secondhand and out-of-print
books, some of them in English.

Libreria della Toletta

MAP P.50, POCKET MAP B16
Sacca della Toletta 1214 Ⓦ latoletta.it.
The longest-established bookshop
in Venice, sells reduced-price
books, mainly in Italian,
but some dual-language and
translations; keeps a good stock
of Venice-related books along
with art, architecture, design and
photography titles. Look out too
for events in their Spazio Eventi on
nearby Fondamenta di Borgo.

Paola Rizzo

MAP P.50, POCKET MAP D16
Dorsoduro 697/A Ⓦ paolarizzo.it.
Designed by Paola Rizzo, and
made by her husband Enzo
Toso – the sixteenth in a line of
Murano glassmakers. Beautiful, yet
surprisingly inexpensive jewellery
and a wonderful collection of
subtly coloured sake glasses.

Paolo Olbi

MAP P.50, POCKET MAP B14
Ponte Ca' Fóscari 3253 Ⓦ olbi.atspace.com.
The founder of this bookbindery
and stationery shop was largely
responsible for the revival of paper
marbling in Venice; today Olbi
sells a range of marbled notebooks,
diaries and other paper goods from
his workshop by the entrance to the
main university building.

Perlamadre

MAP P.50, POCKET MAP B15
Calle delle Botteghe 3182
Ⓦ perlamadredesign.com.
Wonderful pieces of bold glass
jewellery made by two artisans in a
tiny Dorsoduro workshop. They also
run workshops where you can learn
to make Venetian glass beads using
the lampwork technique (where the
glass is worked directly in the flame
of a torch called a *cannello*).

Cafés and pasticcerie

Il Caffè

MAP P.50, POCKET MAP A14
Campo S. Margherita 2963 Ⓦ cafferosso.it.
Known as *Caffè Rosso* for its big red
sign, this small, atmospheric, old-

Reproduction of a Carnival mask outside Ca' Macana

fashioned café-bar is a big buzzy favourite all day and well into the evening. Serves good sandwiches, and there are lots of seats outside in the campo. DJ sets some Sundays at aperitivo time. €

Il Doge

MAP P.50, POCKET MAP A15
Campo S. Margherita 3058
Ⓦ facebook.com/ildogegelateria.
Well-established, very friendly and extremely good hole-in-the-wall *gelateria*, which also does a superb granita, made in the traditional Sicilian way. The most famous flavour is Crema di Doge – vanilla with chocolate and candied orange, but take a good look before you choose because they are always inventing new combinations; recent hits include vanilla with fresh raspberry and chocolate, and yogurt with honey and toasted sesame seeds. €

Majer

MAP P.50, POCKET MAP A15
Rio Terà Canal 3108b Ⓦ majer.it.
Founded as a bakery back in 1924, *Majer* has opened this functional yet pleasant café on the south side

of Campo Santa Margherita. Their pastries are as good as their bread, and the coffee is fine. *Majer* has half a dozen other branches in Venice, all different – see website for details. €

Nico

MAP P.50, POCKET MAP D8
Záttere ai Gesuati 922
Ⓦ gelaterianico.com.
This *café-gelateria*, founded in 1937, still has a feel of the 1950s when Peggy Guggenheim was a loyal client, as does its menu of ice cream sundaes – most famously the *gianduiotto*– a block of praline ice cream drowned in whipped cream. It does ordinary cones and coppette as well, to savour on its lovely waterfront terrace or lick as you walk along the Zattere. €

Tonolo

MAP P.50, POCKET MAP B13
Calle San Pantalon 3764 Ⓦ pasticceria-tonolo-venezia.business.site.
One of the busiest cafés on one of the busiest streets of the student district, especially hectic on Sunday mornings, when the renowned *Tonolo* cakes are in high demand.

Don't miss their sweet, almond-encrusted *Focaccia di Venezia* or, in Carnevale season, the traditional mini doughnut-like *frittelle* with raisins and pine-nuts. €

Restaurants

Ai Quattro Feri

MAP P.50, POCKET MAP A15
Calle Lunga S. Barnaba 2754a
☎ 041 520 6978.
A very highly recommended *osteria* just off Campo San Barnaba with a menu that changes daily but often consists entirely of fish and seafood. Booking essential at all times. €€

Bisicchia

MAP P.50, POCKET MAP B6
Fondamenta de L'Arzere 2277.
Sicilian specialties in a student self-service eatery with snacks such as arancini, and full fixed price lunches for less than a vaporetto ticket. Tables outside by the canal. €

La Bitta

MAP P.50, POCKET MAP A15
Calle Lunga S. Barnaba 2753a
Ⓦ facebook.com/LaBittaVenezia.

Intimate place with an innovative daily changing menu that's remarkable for focussing on meat from a local farm. Marcellino runs the kitchen while his wife Debora serves the guests, offering expert guidance on the impressive wine and grappa list. Delicious cheese platter, served with honey and fruit chutney. Two tiny dining rooms and a few tables in the garden in summer; booking essential. €€

La Calcina

MAP P.50, POCKET MAP E8
Záttere ai Gesuati 780 Ⓦ lacalcina.com.
Occupying a terrace built out over the water, the *Calcina* (belonging to a hotel of the same name) is one of the most pleasant restaurants in Dorsoduro. The service is excellent, the food is good, and the view of Giudecca from the terrace is wonderful. €€€

Oniga

MAP P.50, POCKET MAP A15
Campo S. Barnaba 2852 Ⓦ oniga.it.
One of several good mid-range restaurants in the San Barnaba area, is best known for its Bucintoro menu – first comes a

Handmade pieces at Il Grifone

huge pan of seafood in sauce with crostini, then, once you have eaten most of the seafood, the waiter adds steaming spaghetti to soak up the juices. €€

Trattoria Anzolo Raffaele

MAP P.50, POCKET MAP B7
Campo dell'Anzolo Raffaele, 1722
Dorsoduro Ⓦ trattoriaanzoloraffaele.it.
Combining Venetian and Sardinian traditions on one of the quietest squares in Venice, this traditional-looking trattoria sources vegetables from Sant'Erasmo, and serves dishes you won't find anywhere else such as ravioli with ricotta, saffron and orange zest, or (in autumn) a kind of lasagne called pasticiata with squash, chanterelles and smoked cheese. Desserts are a great feature (try the apple crumble with ice cream), made by the chef's wife, and there is a lovely range of wines by the glass. €€

Bars and snacks

Café Noir

MAP P.50, POCKET MAP B13
Crosera 3805 Ⓣ 041 200 7893.
A favourite student bar serving well-priced cocktails. There is often live music here. €

Cantina del Vino già Schiavi

MAP P.50, POCKET MAP B16
Fondamenta Nani 992 Ⓦ cantinaschiavi.com.
Known to Venetians as the *Cantinone* or *Al Bottegon*, this is a great and long-established bar and wine shop, on the other side of the canal from San Trovaso church. Excellent *cicheti* and generously filled panini too. €

Da Còdroma

MAP P.50, POCKET MAP C6
Fondamenta Briati 2540
Ⓦ facebook.com/dacodroma.
Perennially popular with Venice's students and with people of

all ages from the surrounding parishes, this wood-panelled *osteria* has refectory-style tables and serves simple meals, but most of the punters are just here for a glass, a snack and a chat. It hosts occasional poetry readings and live jazz as well. €€

Impronta Cafè

MAP P.50, POCKET MAP B13
Calle Crosera San Pantalon 3815
Ⓦ improntacafevenice.com.
Impronta Cafè is a distinctively bright, stylish and youthful bar-café-restaurant that is busy at all hours of the day. Drop in for a quick morning coffee, come in to enjoy an evening spritz or even settle down with a nightcap, or sit down for a full meal – the menu changes daily. €€

Margaret DuChamp

MAP P.50, POCKET MAP A14
Campo S. Margherita 3019
Ⓦ camposantamargherita.com/bar.htm.
Lively bar popular with style-conscious Venetians and students, with plenty of seats out on the campo for much of the year. €

Osteria alla Bifora

MAP P.50, POCKET MAP A14
Campo S. Margherita 2930
Ⓦ facebook.com/100054338148909.
With a candlelit, wood-beamed and brick interior, friendly service, good wine, excellent *cicheti*, and spit-roast suckling pig with potatoes if you are really hungry, the *Osteria Alla Bifora* is one of several fine places to dawdle on Campo di Santa Margherita. €

Vinus Venezia

MAP P.50, POCKET MAP B13
Calle del Scaleter 3961 Ⓦ vinusvenezia.it.
A bijou and very pleasant wine bar near San Rocco; the stock of wines here isn't huge, but you will find that the selection has certainly been chosen with care, and the panini are succulent. €

San Polo and Santa Croce

The focal points of daily life in San Polo and Santa Croce are the sociable open space of Campo San Polo and the bustling Rialto area, commercial heart of the Republic and still the home of a market that's famous far beyond the city's boundaries. The hubbub of the stalls and the bars are a good antidote to cultural overload. Life is lived at a far slower pace in Santa Croce, with squares like Campo San Cassian, Campo Maria Mater Domini and Campo San Giacomo dell'Orio still retaining a neighbourhood feel. The major sights here are the extraordinary pair of buildings in the southern part of San Polo: the colossal Gothic church of the Frari and the Scuola Grande di San Rocco, decorated with an unforgettable cycle of paintings by Tintoretto. In the northern part of the district, Venice's modern art, oriental and natural history museums are clustered together on the bank of the Canal Grande: the first two collections occupy one of the city's most magnificent palaces. As ever, numerous treasures are also scattered among the minor churches, notably San Cassiano, San Giovanni Elemosinario and San Simeone Profeta.

The Rialto

MAP P.64, POCKET MAP E11–F12

Relatively stable building land and a good defensive position drew some of the earliest lagoon settlers to the high bank (*rivo alto*) that was to develop into the Rialto district. As the political centre of Venice grew around San Marco, the Rialto became the commercial area. In the twelfth century Europe's first state bank was opened here, and the financiers of this quarter were to be the heavyweights of the international currency exchanges for the next three hundred years and more. And through the **markets of the Rialto** Venice earned a reputation as the bazaar of Europe. Trading had been going on here for over four hundred years when, in the winter of 1514, a fire destroyed everything in the area except the church. Reconstruction began almost straight away: the **Fabbriche Vecchie di Rialto** (the

arcaded buildings along the Ruga degli Orefici and around the Campo San Giacomo) were finished eight years after the fire, with Sansovino's **Fabbriche Nuove di Rialto** (running along the Canal Grande) following about thirty years later.

Today's Rialto market is tamer than that of Venice at its peak, but it's still one of the liveliest spots in the city. You'll find fruit sellers, vegetable stalls, cheese kiosks, a number of good *alimentari* and some fine bars and *osterie* here. The Rialto market is open Monday to Saturday mornings with a few stalls opening again later in the afternoon; the arcaded **Pescheria** (fish market) is closed on Monday as well. It is well worth arriving early to see the produce arriving by boat.

San Giacomo di Rialto

MAP P.64, POCKET MAP F12

Campo S. Giacomo di Rialto.

Venetian legend asserts that the city was founded at noon on Friday, March 25, 421; from the same legend derives the claim that the church of San Giacomo di Rialto, or San Giacometto, was consecrated in that year, and is thus the oldest church in Venice; it was, however, rebuilt in 1071. Parts of the present structure date from this period – the interior's six columns of ancient Greek marble have eleventh-century Veneto-Byzantine capitals – and it seems likely that the reconstruction of the church prompted the establishment of the market here.

Il Gobbo

MAP P.64, POCKET MAP E12
Campo S. Giacomo di Rialto.
On the opposite side of the campo from the church crouches a stone figure known as Il Gobbo di Rialto or the Rialto hunchback. It supports a granite platform from which state proclamations were read simultaneously with their announcement from the Pietra del Bando, beside San Marco; it had another role as well – certain wrongdoers were sentenced to run the gauntlet, stark naked, from the Piazza to the Gobbo.

San Giovanni Elemosinario

MAP P.64, POCKET MAP E12
Ruga Vecchia San Giovanni
Ⓦ **chorusvenezia.org. Charge.**
The church of San Giovanni Elemosinario is so solidly packed into the surrounding buildings that its campanile is the only conspicuous indication of its presence. Founded in the eleventh century, it was wrecked in the huge Rialto fire of 1514 – only the campanile survived – and rebuilt in 1527–29. Most of the church's decoration dates from the decades immediately following the rebuild; the best artworks are **Titian**'s high altarpiece of *St John the Almsgiver*, and **Pordenone**'s nearby *SS Catherine, Sebastian and Roch*. The frescoes in the cupola, featuring a gang of very chunky cherubs, are also by Pordenone.

San Cassiano

MAP P.64, POCKET MAP D11
Calle dei Morti.
The thirteenth-century campanile is the only appealing aspect of

Seller at Rialto market

and *The Crucifixion*. The third is one of the most startling pictures in Venice – centred on the ladder on which the executioners stand, it's painted as though the observer were lying in the grass at the foot of the Cross.

Campo San Cassiano was the site of the **first public opera house** in the world – it opened in 1636, at the peak of Monteverdi's career. Long into the following century Venice's opera houses were among the most active in Europe; around five hundred works received their first performances here in the first half of the eighteenth century.

Campo Santa Maria Mater Domini

MAP P.64, POCKET MAP D11

The small Campo Santa Maria Mater Domini is a perfect Venetian miscellany, untouched by tourism – a thirteenth-century house (the Casa Zane), a few ramshackle

The Ca' Pésaro on the Grand Canal

the exterior of the church of San Cassiano, but inside there are three fine paintings by **Tintoretto**: *The Resurrection*, *The Descent into Limbo*

San Polo and Santa Croce

Gothic houses, an assortment of stone reliefs of indeterminate age, a fourteenth-century wellhead in the centre, a workaday bar, a couple of shops, and a hairdresser. The church of **Santa Maria Mater Domini**, a handsome early sixteenth-century building, boasts an endearing *Martyrdom of St Christina* by **Vincenzo Catena**, showing a flight of angels plucking the saint from a carpet-like Lago di Bolsena, into which she had been hurled with a millstone for an anchor.

Ca' Pésaro

MAP P.64, POCKET MAP D10–11
Santa Croce 2076 Ⓦ capesaro.visitmuve.it. Charge.

The immense Ca' Pésaro was bequeathed to the city at the end of the nineteenth century by the Duchessa Felicità Bevilacqua La Masa who stipulated in her will that it should provide

accommodation for impoverished young artists. Adventurous shows were staged here for a while, but instead of becoming a permanent centre for the living arts the palazzo has become home to the **Galleria Internazionale d'Arte Moderna**. The name is slightly misleading: a few of the foreign heavyweights of modern art are here (eg Klimt, Kandinsky, Matisse, Klee, Picasso, Ernst and Miró), but in essence this is a very selective overview of Italian art in the late nineteenth and twentieth centuries. The top-floor rooms are home to the **Museo Orientale** (Ⓦ orientalevenezia. beniculturali.it, charge), a tightly packed array of porcelain, armour, musical instruments, clothing, and enough weaponry to equip a private army. Many of the pieces are exquisite – look out for an incredibly intricate chess set, and a room full of marvellous lacquerwork.

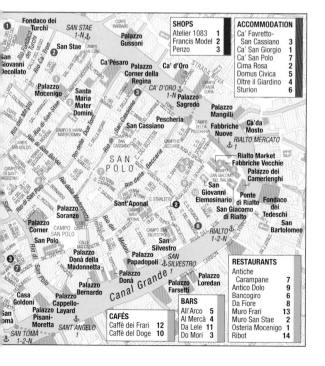

San Stae

MAP P.64, POCKET MAP D10
Salizada San Stae
Ⓦ chorusvenezia.org. Charge.

Continuing along the line of the
Canal Grande from the Ca' Pésaro,
Calle Pésaro takes you over the
Rio della Rioda, and so to the
seventeenth-century church of
San Stae. Its Baroque facade is
enlivened by precarious statues, and
the *marmorino* (pulverized marble)
surfaces of the interior make San
Stae as bright as an operating theatre
on sunny days. In the chancel
there's a series of paintings from the
beginning of the eighteenth century,
the pick of which are *The Martyrdom
of St James the Great* by Piazzetta
(low on the left), *The Liberation
of St Peter* by Sebastiano Ricci
(same row) and *The Martyrdom of
St Bartholomew* by Giambattista
Tiepolo (opposite). Exhibitions and
concerts are often held in San Stae.

Palazzo Mocenigo

MAP P.64, POCKET MAP C11
Santa Croce 1992
Ⓦ mocenigo.visitmuve.it. Charge.

Halfway down the alley flanking San
Stae is the early seventeenth-century
Palazzo Mocenigo, now home to a
centre for the study of textiles and
clothing. The library and archive of
the study centre occupy part of the
building, but a substantial portion
of the *piano nobile* is open to the

public, and there are few Venetian
interiors of this date that have been
so meticulously preserved: the
rooms are full of portraits, antique
furniture, Murano chandeliers and
display cases of dandified clothing
and cobweb-fine lacework.

The curtains are kept closed
to protect such delicate items as
floral silk stockings, silvery padded
waistcoats, and an extraordinarily
embroidered outfit once worn by
what must have been the best-
dressed 5 year old in town.

San Giovanni Decollato

MAP P.64, POCKET MAP C10
Campo San Zan Degolà.

The signposted route to the train
station passes the deconsecrated
church of San Giovanni Decollato,
or San Zan Degolà in dialect – it
means "St John the Beheaded".
Established in the opening years
of the eleventh century, it has
retained its layout through several
alterations; the columns and
capitals of the nave date from the
first century of its existence, and
parts of its fragmentary **frescoes**
(at the east end) may be of the
same age. Some of the paintings are
certainly thirteenth century, and no
other church in Venice has frescoes
that predate them. The church also
has one of the city's characteristic
ship's-keel ceilings. It now hosts the
city's Russian Orthodox church.

Who's San Stae?

Among the chief characteristics of the **Venetian vernacular**
are its tendencies to slur consonants, abbreviate syllables and
swallow vowels. For example, the Italian name Giuseppe here
becomes Isepo, Giuliano becomes Zulian, Eustachio becomes
Stae, Biagio becomes Biasio (or Blasio), Agostino shrinks to Stin,
and Giovanni is Zuan or Zan – as in San Zan Degolà, for San
Giovanni Decollato.

You'll also see *dose* instead of *doge*, *do* instead of *due*, *nove*
instead of *nuove* and *fontego* for *fondaco*. And you may notice, too,
that the letter "x" occasionally replaces "z" (as in the example
of *venexiana*), and that the final vowel is habitually lopped off
Venetian surnames, as in Giustinian, Loredan and Vendramin, to
cite just three of the most conspicuous instances.

The San Zan Degolà church, or San Giovanni Decollato

The Museo Storico Naturale

MAP P.64, POCKET MAP C10
Fondaco dei Turchi Ⓦ msn.visitmuve.it. Charge.

The Museo di Storia Naturale is located inside the Fondaco dei Turchi. The fossil collection is displayed with great imagination, and you'll also find an extraordinary miscellany of items gathered by Giovanni Miani during his 1859–60 expedition to trace the source of the Nile, along with the 18.60m long skeleton of a fin-back whale washed up on the shore near Naples in 1928, an excellent reconstruction of a Wunderkammer or Cabinet of Curiosities and an aquarium which replicates the ecosystem of the tegnùe, the coral reef of the Adriatic – the best example of which is just off the coast of Chioggia. It's a huge and fascinating collection, but the captions are in Italian only.

San Giacomo dell'Orio

MAP P.64, POCKET MAP B11
Campo San Giacomo dell'Orio
Ⓦ chorusvenezia.org. Charge.

Standing in a lovely campo which, despite its size, you could easily miss if you weren't looking for it, San Giacomo dell'Orio is an ancient and atmospheric church. Founded in the ninth century (the shape of the apse betrays its Byzantine origins), it was rebuilt in 1225 and remodelled on numerous subsequent occasions, notably when its **ship's-keel roof** was added in the fourteenth century. Several fine paintings are displayed here. The main altarpiece, *Madonna and Four Saints*, was painted by Lorenzo Lotto in 1546, shortly before he left the city complaining that the Venetians had not treated him fairly; the Crucifix that hangs in the air in front of it is attributed to Paolo Veneziano. In the left transept there's an altarpiece by Paolo Veronese, and there's a fine set of pictures from Veronese's workshop on the ceiling of the **new sacristy**. The **old sacristy** is a showcase for the art of Palma il Giovane, whose cycle in celebration of the Eucharist covers the walls and part of the ceiling.

San Simeone Profeta

MAP P.64, POCKET MAP A11
Campiello S. Simeone Grande.

Originating in the tenth century, the church of San Simeone Profeta (or Grande) has often been rebuilt – most extensively in the eighteenth century, when the city sanitation experts, anxious about the condition of the plague victims who had been buried under the flagstones in the 1630 epidemic, ordered the whole floor to be relaid. Though undistinguished as a building, it's remarkable for its reclining **effigy of St Simeon** (to the left of the chancel), a luxuriantly bearded, larger than lifesize figure, whose half-open mouth disturbingly creates the impression of the moment of death. According to its inscription, it was sculpted in 1317 by **Marco Romano**, but some experts doubt that the sculpture can be that old, as nothing else of that date bears comparison with it.

Campo San Polo

MAP P.64, POCKET MAP C12
South of the Rialto, **Ruga Vecchia San Giovanni** constitutes the first leg of the right bank's nearest equivalent to the Mercerie of San Marco, a reasonably straight chain of shop-lined alleyways that's interrupted by Campo San Polo, the largest square in Venice after the Piazza. In earlier times it was the site of weekly markets and occasional fairs, as well as being used as a parade ground and bullfighting arena. And on one occasion Campo San Polo was the scene of a bloody act of political retribution: on February 26, 1548, Lorenzaccio de'Medici, having fled Florence after murdering the deranged duke Alessandro (a distant relative and former friend), was murdered here by assassins sent by Duke Cosimo I, Alessandro's successor.

San Polo

MAP P.64, POCKET MAP C13
Campo San Polo Ⓦ chorusvenezia.org. Charge.

The bleak interior of San Polo church is worth a visit for a *Last Supper* by Tintoretto (on the left as you enter) and a cycle of the *Stations of the Cross* (*Via Crucis*) by Giandomenico Tiepolo in the Oratory of the Crucifix (entrance under organ). This powerful series, painted when the artist was only 20, appears less frivolous than Giandomenico customarily is, even if some of the scenes do feature lustrously attired sophisticates who seem to have drifted in from the salons of eighteenth-century Venice. A couple of Tiepolo ceiling panels and two other easel paintings supplement the *Via Crucis*; back in the main part of the church, paintings by Giandomenico's father and Veronese are displayed on the second altar opposite the door and in the chapel on the left of the chancel respectively, but neither shows the artist at his best.

Casa Goldoni

MAP P.64, POCKET MAP C13
Calle dei Nomboli 2794
Ⓦ carlogoldoni.visitmuve.it. Charge.

The fifteenth-century **Palazzo Centani** was the birthplace of **Carlo Goldoni** (1707–93), the playwright who transformed the *commedia dell'arte* from a vehicle for semi-improvised clowning into a medium for sharp political observation. Goldoni's plays are still the staple of theatrical life in Venice, and there's no risk of running out of material – allegedly he once bet a friend that he could produce one play a week for a whole year, and won. Goldoni's home now houses a theatre studies institute and the **Museo Goldoni**, a very small collection of first editions, portraits and theatrical paraphernalia, including some eighteenth-century marionettes and a miniature theatre.

Santa Maria Gloriosa dei Frari

MAP P.64, POCKET MAP B13
Campo dei Frari ⓦ basilicadeifrari.it.
Charge.

Santa Maria Gloriosa dei Frari – always abbreviated to the **Frari** – was founded by the Franciscans around 1250, not long after the death of their founder, but almost no sooner was the first church completed (in 1338) than work began on a vast replacement, a project which took well over a hundred years. The campanile, one of the city's landmarks and the tallest after San Marco's, was finished in 1396.

You're unlikely to fall in love at first sight with this mountain of brick, but the outside of the church is a misleadingly dull prelude to an astounding interior. Apart from the Accademia and the Salute, the Frari is the only building in Venice with more than a single first-rate work by **Titian**, and one of these – the **Assumption** – you'll see right away, as it soars over the high altar. It's a piece of compositional and colouristic bravura for which there was no precedent in Venetian art (no previous altarpiece had so emphasized the vertical axis), and the other Titian masterpiece here, the **Madonna di Ca'Pésaro** (on the left wall, between the third and fourth columns), was equally innovative in its displacement of the figure of the Virgin from the centre of the picture. Other paintings to look out for are Bartolomeo Vivarini's *St Mark Enthroned* (in the Cappella Corner, at the end of the left transept); Alvise Vivarini's *St Ambrose and other Saints* (in the adjoining chapel, where you'll also find the grave of Monteverdi); and, above all, **Giovanni Bellini**'s serene and solemn *Madonna and Child with SS. Nicholas of Bari, Peter, Mark and Benedict*, in the **sacristy**.

Apart from its paintings, the Frari is also remarkable for **Donatello**'s luridly naturalistic wooden statue *St John the Baptist* (in the chapel to the right of the transept), the beautiful fifteenth-century monks' choir, and its wealth of extravagant tombs. Two of the finest monuments flank the Titian *Assumption*: on the left is the proto-Renaissance **tomb of Doge Niccolò Tron**, by Antonio Rizzo and assistants (1476); on the right, the more archaic and chaotic **tomb of Doge Francesco Fóscari**, carved shortly after Fóscari's death in 1457 (after 34 years as doge) by Antonio and Paolo Bregno.

Against the right-hand wall of the nave stands the house-sized **monument to Titian**, built in the mid-nineteenth century on the supposed place of his burial. The artist died in 1576, in around his ninetieth year, a casualty of the plague; such was the esteem in which Titian was held, he was the only victim to be allowed a church burial in the course of the outbreak. The marble pyramid on the opposite side of the church is the

Campo San Polo

Interior of Santa Maria Gloriosa dei Frari

Mausoleum of Canova, erected by pupils of the sculptor, following a design he himself had made for the tombs of Titian and Maria Christina of Austria. Finally, you can't fail to notice what is surely the most grotesque monument in the city, the tomb of **Doge Giovanni Pésaro** (1669), held aloft by gigantic ragged-trousered Moors and decomposing corpses.

The Scuola Grande di San Rocco

MAP P.64, POCKET MAP B13
Campo San Rocco
Ⓦ scuolagrandesanrocco.it. Charge.
Unless you've been to the Scuola Grande di San Rocco you can't properly appreciate the genius of Tintoretto. Ruskin called it "one of the three most precious buildings in Italy", and it's not difficult to understand why he resorted to such hyperbole. (His other votes were for the Sistine Chapel and the Camposanto at Pisa; the latter was badly damaged in World War

II.) The unremitting concentration and restlessness of Tintoretto's paintings won't inspire unqualified enthusiasm in everyone, but even those who prefer their art at a lower voltage should find this an astounding experience.

From its foundation in 1478, the special concern of this particular *scuola* was the relief of the sick – a continuation of the Christian mission of its patron saint, St Roch (Rocco) of Montpellier, who in 1315 left his home town to work among plague victims in Italy. The Scuola had been going for seven years when the body of the saint was brought to Venice from Germany, and the consequent boom in donations was so great that in 1489 it acquired the status of *scuola grande*. In 1527 the city was hit by an outbreak of plague, and the Scuola's revenue rocketed to record levels as gifts poured in from people hoping to secure St Roch's protection against the disease. The fattened coffers paid for this building, and for **Tintoretto**'s amazing cycle of more than fifty major paintings.

The narrative sequence begins with the first picture in the lower room – the *Annunciation*. But to appreciate Tintoretto's development you have to begin in the smaller room on the upper storey – the **Sala dell'Albergo**. This is dominated by the stupendous *Crucifixion* (1565), the most compendious image of the event ever painted. Tintoretto's other works here – aside from the *Glorification of St Roch* in the middle of the ceiling (the piece that won him the contract to decorate the whole room) – are on the entrance wall.

Tintoretto finished his contribution to the Sala dell'Albergo in 1567. Eight years later, when the Scuola decided to proceed with the embellishment of the main upper hall – the **chapter house** – he undertook to do the work in return for nothing more than his expenses. In the event he was awarded a lifetime annuity, and then commenced the **ceiling**. The Scuola's governors were so pleased with these three large panels that he was given the task of decorating the entire interior – a feat of sustained inventiveness that has few equals in Western art. Though he was in his late sixties when he came to paint the **lower hall**, there is no sign of flagging creativity: indeed, the landscapes in *The Flight into Egypt* and the meditative depictions of *St Mary Magdalen* and *St Mary of Egypt* are among the finest he ever created.

The church of San Rocco

MAP P.64, POCKET MAP B13
Campo San Rocco.

Before or after a visit to the neighbouring Scuola of San Rocco, pop into the church of San Rocco, where – on the right wall of the nave – you'll find *St Roch Taken to Prison*, and below it *The Pool of Bethesda*; the latter is definitely by Tintoretto, the former possibly by him. Between the altars on the other side are a couple of good pictures by **Pordenone** – *St Christopher* and *St Martin*. Four large paintings by Tintoretto hang in the chancel, often either lost in the gloom or glazed with sunlight: the best (both painted in 1549) are *St Roch Curing the Plague Victims* (lower right) and *St Roch in Prison* (lower left).

The Scuola di San Giovanni Evangelista

MAP P.64, POCKET MAP B12
Calle de la Laca ⓦ scuolasangiovanni.it.

The Scuola di San Giovanni Evangelista, which nestles in a line of drab buildings near to the Frari, was founded in 1261 and its finest hour came in 1369 when it was presented with a relic of the True Cross. The miracles effected by the relic were commemorated in a series of paintings by Carpaccio,

Gentile Bellini and others, now in the Accademia. The interior is open to the public (visiting hours are posted monthly on the website, and guided tours in English are sometimes available), but the chief attraction of the Scuola is the superb screen of the outer courtyard; built in 1481 by Pietro Lombardo, it's a wonderfully delicate piece of marble carving.

The Tolentini

MAP P.64, POCKET MAP C5
Campo dei Tolentini.

The portentous church of San Nicolò da Tolentino – alias dei Tolentini – was the Venetian home of the Theatine Order, which found refuge in Venice after the Sack of Rome by the army of Charles V in 1527. It was begun in 1590 by Palladio's follower Scamozzi, and finished in 1714 by the addition of a freestanding portico – the first in Venice – designed by Andrea Tirali.

Among scores of seventeenth-century paintings here, two stand out. The first is a *St Jerome* by Johann Lys, at the foot of the chancel steps, on the left; it was painted in 1628, just two years before German-born Lys died of the plague, aged 33. The other is *St Lawrence Giving Alms* by Bernardo Strozzi, round the corner from the Lys painting, to the left. Up the left wall of the chancel swirls the best Baroque monument in Venice: the **tomb of Francesco Morosini**, the Patriach of Venice, created in 1678 by a Genoese sculptor, Filippo Parodi.

The Giardino Papadopoli

MAP P.64, POCKET MAP C4–5
Fondamenta Papadopoli.

If fatigue is setting in and you need a pit-stop, make for the nearby Giardino Papadopoli, which is just over the Rio dei Tolentini. Formerly one of Venice's biggest private gardens, it is now owned by the city.

Shops

Atelier 1083

MAP P.64, POCKET MAP B11
Ruga Bella 1083A Santa Croce
Ⓦ atelier1083a.com.
Inventive contemporary hand-made porcelain and wood by partners Diana and Gabriele. Diana's delicate porcelain tableware takes on organic forms inspired by the sea and the fruit and veg of Rialto market, while Gabriele creates furniture and objects both useful and aesthetic from old bricole – the iconic oak posts of the lagoon – and waste wood from the parks and gardens of Venice where he works as a gardener.

Francis Model

MAP P.64, POCKET MAP E12
Ruga Vecchia San Giovanni 773
Ⓦ francismodel.it.
This father-and-son workshop produces high-quality handbags and briefcases.

Penzo

MAP P.64, POCKET MAP C13
Calle Seconda Saoneri 2681
Ⓦ veniceboats.com.
For a uniquely Venetian gift, call in at Gilberto Penzo's shop, which sells models, model kits and elegantly drawn plans of Venetian boats, from gondolas to vaporetti. For anyone interested in maritime history the website is a treasure chest of information.

Cafés

Caffè dei Frari

MAP P.64, POCKET MAP B13
Calle del Scaleter 2564
Ⓦ facebook.com/100063727321644.
Very atmospheric and pretty Belle Époque-styled bar-café opposite the Frari's front door. Delicious and beautifully presented crostini and crisp slices of polenta topped with chicken liver. €

Caffè del Doge

MAP P.64, POCKET MAP E12
Calle dei Cinque 609 Ⓦ caffedeldoge.com.
Fantastically good coffee created by a *torrefazione* (coffee-roaster) founded in 1952, served in a chic minimalist bar very close to the Rialto Bridge. €

Restaurants

Antiche Carampane

MAP P.64, POCKET MAP D12
Rio Terrà delle Carampane 1911
Ⓦ antichecarampane.com.
If not the most tourist-friendly place in the city (a semi-jokey notice that tells you there's "No lasagne, no pizza, no menu turistico"), the *Carampane* is a thoroughbred Venetian trattoria, serving excellent seafood in a cosy interior – with outside seating in fine weather. The brief menu is often wholly fish-based. €€€

Antico Dolo

MAP P.64, POCKET MAP E12
Ruga Rialto San Giovanni 778 Ⓦ anticodolo.it.
You can pop into this excellent, long-established *osteria* for a few *cicheti* and a glass of Merlot and come away just a few euros poorer; or you can take a table and eat an excellent meal without breaking the bank. €€

Bancogiro

MAP P.64, POCKET MAP F12
Sottoportego del Banco Giro 122
Ⓦ osteriabancogiro.it.
Very popular *osteria*, in a splendid location in the midst of the Rialto market. Come here to nurse a glass of fine wine beside the Canal Grande, or nip upstairs to the dining room for the likes of black bigoli with mussels, harissa and bottarga or linguine with rabbit ragout, peppers and thyme. €€

Da Fiore

MAP P.64, POCKET MAP C12
Calle del Scaleter 2202a
Ⓦ ristorantedafiore.com.

Hyper-refined *Da Fiore* is possibly the most famous restaurant in Venice, and is certainly one of the most lauded, both by Italians and foreign foodies. If you're going to treat yourself here, make sure you book well in advance to reserve one of the two canalside tables on the tiny terrace. €€€€

Muro San Stae

MAP P.64, POCKET MAP C11 & C13
Campiello del Spezier 2048–50
Ⓦ murovenezia.com.
Muro has an imaginative seafood menu and a lovely selection of risotto and pasta. The styling is spartan, the service excellent and there is seating outside. *Muro Frari*, at Rio Terrà dei Frari 2604, has a menu aimed at more gastronomical conservative travellers (simple pasta dishes and lots of steaks). €€

Osteria Mocenigo

MAP P.64, POCKET MAP C11
Salizzada S.Stae 1919 Ⓣ 041 523 1703.
Cosy, cheery and popular neighbourhood trattoria serving decent inexpensive Venetian staples – try the black spaghetti with prawns or a fish risotto. House wine by the carafe. €

Ribot

MAP P.64, POCKET MAP G4
Fondamenta Minotto 158
Ⓦ ristoranteribot.business.site.
Named after a famous racehorse (in case you're wondering about the logo), *Ribot* is an old-fashioned, good-value restaurant, with a menu that draws on recipes from beyond the Veneto, and has a lovely garden out back. There are some well-priced set menus. €€

Bars and snacks

All'Arco

MAP P.64, POCKET MAP E12
Calle del'Ochialer 436 Ⓣ 041 520 5666.
A great stand-up Rialto bar, tucked under the end of the sottoportego

opposite S. Giovanni Elemosinario; does superb *sarde in saor* and other snacks. €

Al Mercà

MAP P.64, POCKET MAP E12
Campo Cesare Battisti 213 Ⓣ 346 834 0660.
This minuscule stand-up Rialto bar is perfect for a quick and authentic *panino* and ombra or prosecco. €

Da Lele

MAP P.64, POCKET MAP C5
Campo dei Tolentini 183.
This tiny and utterly authentic early-opening stand-up bar attracts a lot of custom from workers en route to or from Piazzale Roma. Sandwiches and rolls made freshly to order; wine by the glass is so cheap you will think the bartender has made a mistake. €

Do Mori

MAP P.64, POCKET MAP E12
Calle Do Mori 429 Ⓣ 041 5225401.
Hidden just off Ruga Vecchia S. Giovanni, *Do Mori* is one of the city's most authentic old-style Venetian bars. It's a single narrow room, with no seating, packed every evening with shopworkers, Rialto porters and locals just out for a stroll. Delicious snacks, good range of wines, terrific atmosphere. €

Food at *Antiche Carampane*

Cannaregio

Don't be put off by the hustle around the train station – in Cannaregio, Venice's northernmost section, it's very easy to get well away from the tourist crowds as you explore the area's enticing backwaters. The pleasures of this *sestiere* are generally more a matter of atmosphere than of specific sights, but you shouldn't leave Venice without seeing the Ghetto, the first area in the world to bear that name and one of Venice's most evocative quarters, or without spending an evening checking out the bars and restaurants of lively Fondamenta dei Ormesini. There are some special buildings to visit too: Madonna dell'Orto, with its astonishing Tintoretto paintings; Sant'Alvise and the Palazzo Labia, both remarkable for works by Giambattista Tiepolo; the Ca' d'Oro, a gorgeous Canal Grande palace housing a sizeable art collection; the highly photogenic Santa Maria dei Miracoli; and the Gesuiti, a Baroque creation which boasts perhaps the weirdest interior in the city.

The Scalzi and the Giardino Mistico

MAP P.76, POCKET MAP C3
Rio Terà Lista di Spagna
Ⓦ chiesadegliscalzi.it. Free.

Right by the station stands the Scalzi (formally Santa Maria di Nazaretta), which was begun in 1672 for the barefoot ("scalzi") order of Carmelites, but is anything but barefoot itself – the opulent interior is plated with dark, multicoloured marble and overgrown with Baroque statuary. Before an Austrian bomb plummeted through the roof in 1915 there was a great **Giambattista Tiepolo** ceiling here; a few scraps are preserved in the Accademia, and some wan frescoes by Tiepolo survive in the first chapel on the left and the second on the right. The second chapel on the left is the resting place of **Lodovico Manin** (d.1802), Venice's last doge. Across the way is one of Venice's best kept secrets, the Carmelite brothers' Giardino Mistico. It is best known for its Acqua di Melissa, a distillation of *melissa officianalis* and several other herbs, said to be efficacious for ailments ranging from stomach ache to dandruff. The garden does not only grow melissa; there are vegetables too, an orchard dedicated to 'forgotten fruit' with 40 rare varieties of stone fruit. There is even a vineyard in which 21 ancient indigenous grape varietals are cultivated. Surplus fruit and vegetables (when available) and Acqua di Melissa are sold in the convent's little shop. The gardens can be seen by booking ahead on Ⓦ giardinomistico.it.

San Geremia

MAP P.76, POCKET MAP D3
Campo San Geremia Ⓦ santuariodilucia.it.

The church of San Geremia is where the travels of **St Lucy** eventually terminated – martyred in Syracuse in 304, she was stolen from Constantinople by Venetian Crusaders in 1204, then ousted from her own church in Venice in the mid-nineteenth century, when it was demolished to make way for the train station. Her desiccated body, wearing a lustrous silver mask, lies behind the altar, reclining above a donations box that bears the prayer "Saint Lucy, protect my eyes" – she's the patron saint of eyesight (and artists). Nothing else about the church is of interest, except the twelfth-century **campanile**, one of the oldest left in the city.

Palazzo Labia

MAP P.76, POCKET MAP D3
Campo San Geremia Ⓦ rai.it.

The Palazzo Labia, next door to San Geremia, was built in 1720–50 for a famously extravagant Catalan family by the name of Lasbias. No sooner was the interior completed than **Giambattista Tiepolo** was hired to cover the walls of the ballroom with **frescoes** depicting the story of Anthony and Cleopatra. RAI, the Italian state broadcasting company, now owns the palace, but they sometimes allow visitors in for a few hours each week.

San Giobbe

MAP P.76, POCKET MAP C2
Campo San Giobbe Ⓦ chorusvenezia.org. Charge.

Dedicated to Job, whose sufferings greatly endeared him to the Venetians (who were regularly afflicted with malaria, plague and a plethora of water-related diseases), the church is interesting mainly for its exquisitely carved doorway and chancel – the first Venetian projects of **Pietro Lombardo**. The best paintings – a fine triptych by Antonio Vivarini and a *Marriage of St Catherine* attributed to Andrea Previtali – are in the **sacristy**, along with a fifteenth-century terracotta bust of the great preacher St Bernardine, who in 1443 was a guest here (in what turned out to be the last year of his life) and whose canonization in 1450 was marked by the rebuilding of this church.

The Ghetto

MAP P.76, POCKET MAP D2
Campo del Ghetto Nuovo
Ⓦ ghettovenezia.com. Charge.

The name of the Venetian Ghetto – a name bequeathed to all other

View of the San Geremia church

such enclaves of oppression – is probably derived from the Venetian dialect *geto*, foundry, which is what this area used to be. The creation of the Ghetto was a consequence of the War of the League of Cambrai, when hundreds of Jews fled the mainland in fear of the Imperial army. Gaining safe haven in Venice, many of the fugitives donated funds for the defence of the city, and were rewarded with permanent protection – at a price. In 1516 the **Ghetto Nuovo** became Venice's Jewish quarter, when all the city's Jews were forced to move here. At night the Ghetto was sealed by gates, yet Venice was markedly liberal by the standards of the time, and the Ghetto's population was often swelled by refugees from less tolerant societies – indeed, the Jewish population soon spread into the **Ghetto Vecchio** and the **Ghetto Nuovissimo**. The gates of the Ghetto were finally torn down

by Napoleon in 1797, but it wasn't until the unification of Italy that Jews achieved equal status with their fellow citizens.

Each wave of Jewish immigrants maintained their own synagogues with their distinctive rites: the **Scola Tedesca** (for German Jews) was founded in 1528, the **Scola al Canton** (probably Jews from Provence) in 1531–32, the **Scola Levantina** (eastern Mediterranean) in 1538, the **Scola Spagnola** (Spanish) at an uncertain date in the later sixteenth century, and the **Scola Italiana** in 1575. Funded by particularly prosperous trading communities, the Scola Levantina and the Scola Spagnola are the most lavish of the synagogues, and are the only two still used on a daily basis.

Both can be visited, in an informative English-language guided tour by a member of the Jewish community, or with a

Cannaregio

BARS, CAFÉS & GELATERIE

Al Parlamento	7
Bacaro al Gelato	10
Combo Bacaro	12
Dolceamaro	18
Sulla Luna	8
Torrefazione e Cannaregio	2
Un Mondo di Vino	19
Volpe	6

RESTAURANTS

Ai Promessi Sposi	17
Alla Fontana	5
Alla Vedova	15
Anice Stellato	1
Da Rioba	4
Gam Gam	9
Hostaria Bacanera	16
Marcianino	3
Ostaria Santa Fosca	13
Pontini	11
Vini da Gigio	14

self-guided tour. All tours begin in the **Museo Ebraico** where the focus is on personal testimonies and stories aimed at bringing 500 years of Jewish experience in Venice to life. By the time you read this, restoration of German, Canton and Italian synagogues should be complete, and they should also be included in the tours.

Sant'Alvise

MAP P.76, POCKET MAP E1
Campo Sant'Alvise ⓦ chorusvenezia.org. Charge.

Located on the northern periphery of the city, the church of Sant'Alvise is notoriously prone to damp, but restoration has saved the chancel's immense *Road to Calvary* by Giambattista Tiepolo. His *Crown of Thorns* and *Flagellation*, slightly earlier works, hang on the right-hand wall of the nave. Under the nuns' choir you'll find eight small paintings, known as "The

Scola al Canton in the Jewish Ghetto

Baby Carpaccios" since Ruskin assigned them to the painter's precocious childhood; they're not actually by Carpaccio, but they

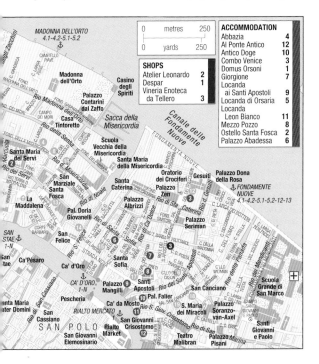

MADONNA DELL'ORTO
4.1-4.2-5.1-5.2

| 0 | metres | 250 |
| 0 | yards | 250 |

SHOPS
Atelier Leonardo   2
Despar   1
Vineria Enoteca
da Tellero   3

ACCOMMODATION
Abbazia   4
Al Ponte Antico   12
Antico Doge   10
Combo Venice   3
Domus Orsoni   1
Giorgione   7
Locanda
  ai Santi Apostoli   9
Locanda di Orsaria   5
Locanda
  Leon Bianco   11
Mezzo Pozzo   8
Ostello Santa Fosca   2
Palazzo Abadessa   6

View of Strada Nova

were produced around 1470, when he would indeed have been just an infant. The extraordinary seventeenth-century trompe l'oeil ceiling is a collaboration between Antonio Torri and Paolo Ricchi. "Alvise", by the way, is the Venetian version of Luigi – the church is dedicated to St Louis of Toulouse.

Madonna dell'Orto

MAP P.76, POCKET MAP F1–2
Campo della Madonna dell'Orto
Ⓦ visitvenezia.eu.

Madonna dell'Orto, the Tintoretto family's parish church, is arguably the finest Gothic church in Venice. Founded in the name of Saint Christopher some time around 1350, it was popularly renamed after a large stone *Madonna* by **Giovanni de'Santi**, found in a nearby vegetable garden (*orto*), began working miracles; brought into the church in 1377, the heavily restored figure now sits in the Cappella di San Mauro (at the end of the right aisle).

Outside, the church is notable for its statue of St Christopher, its elegant portal and its **campanile**, one of the most notable landmarks when approaching Venice from the northern lagoon. Inside, paintings by **Tintoretto** make a massive impact, none more so than the epic picures on each side of the choir: *The Last Judgement* and *The Making of the Golden Calf*. Other paintings by Tintoretto adorn the chancel, but best of all is the tender *Presentation of the Virgin*, at the end of the right aisle, which makes a fascinating comparison with Titian's Accademia version of the incident. A major figure of the early Venetian Renaissance – **Cima da Conegliano** – is represented by a *St John the Baptist and Other Saints*, on the first altar on the right; a *Madonna and Child* by Cima's great contemporary, Giovanni Bellini, used to occupy the first chapel on the left, but thieves made off with it in 1993.

Tintoretto spent the last two decades of his life in a house close to **Campo dei Mori**, to the south of the church. Four thirteenth-century statues stand around the campo: aggrieved citizens used to leave denunciations at the feet of "Sior Antonio Rioba" (the statue with the rusty nose), and circulate vindictive verses signed with his name.

Strada Nova

MAP P.76, POCKET MAP D10–F11

The main land route between the train station and the Rialto Bridge was created in the 1870s by the Austrians. But whereas the Lista di Spagna and Rio Terrà San Leonardo were formed by filling canals with earth, the Strada Nova was created by simply ploughing a line straight through the houses that used to stand here. Outside the church of **Santa Fosca** at the start of Strada Nova, stands a statue of a true Venetian hero, **Fra' Paolo Sarpi**. A brilliant scholar and scientist (he assisted Galileo), Sarpi was the adviser to the Venetian state in its row with the Vatican at the start of the seventeenth century, when the whole city was excommunicated for its refusal to accept papal jurisdiction in secular affairs. One night Sarpi was walking home past Santa Fosca when he was set upon by three men and left for dead with a dagger in his face. "I recognize the style of the Holy See", Sarpi quipped, punning on the word "stiletto". He survived.

Across the Strada Nova, the **Farmacia Ponci** has the oldest surviving shop interior in Venice, a wonderful display of seventeenth-century woodwork in walnut, with eighteenth-century majolica vases.

Ca' d'Oro

MAP P.76, POCKET MAP E10–11

Calle Ca' d'Oro 3932 ⓦ cadoro.org. Charge.

An inconspicuous calle leads down to the Ca' d'Oro (House of Gold), the finest example of domestic Gothic architecture in Venice. Built for procurator Marino Contarini between 1425 and 1440, the palace takes its name from its Canal Grande **facade**: incorporating parts of the thirteenth-century palace that used to stand here, it was highlighted in gold leaf, ultramarine and vermilion – materials which, as the three most expensive pigments of the day,

spectacularly publicized the wealth of its owner. The house's cosmetics have now worn off, but the facade has at least survived unaltered.

Nowadays it's the home of the **Galleria Giorgio Franchetti**, a collection whose main attraction is undoubtedly the *St Sebastian* painted by **Mantegna** shortly before his death in 1506 – it's installed in a chapel-like alcove on the first floor. Many of the big names of Venetian art are found on the second floor, but the canvases by Titian and Tintoretto are not among their best, and Pordenone's fragmentary frescoes from Santo Stefano require a considerable feat of imaginative reconstruction, as do the remains of Giorgione and Titian's work from the Fondaco dei Tedeschi. The Ca' d'Oro's collection of sculpture, though far less extensive than the array of paintings, has more outstanding items, notably **Tullio Lombardo**'s beautifully carved *Young Couple*, and superb portrait busts by Bernini and Alessandro Vittoria. Also arresting are a sixteenth-century English alabaster polyptych of *Scenes from the Life of St Catherine* and a case of Renaissance medals that includes fine specimens by **Gentile Bellini** and **Pisanello**.

Santi Apostoli

MAP P.76, POCKET MAP F11

Campo dei Santi Apostoli

ⓦ museionline.info. Free.

At the eastern end of the Strada you come to the Campo dei Santi Apostoli, an elbow on the road from the Rialto to the train station. The most interesting part of Santi Apostoli church is the **Cappella Corner**, off the right side, where the altarpiece is the *Communion of St Lucy* by Giambattista Tiepolo. One of the inscriptions in the chapel is to Caterina Cornaro, who was buried here before being moved to San Salvatore; the tomb of her father Marco (on the right) is probably by Tullio Lombardo,

CANNAREGIO

who also carved the peculiar plaque of St Sebastian in the chapel to the right of the chancel.

San Giovanni Crisostomo

MAP P.76, POCKET MAP F11
Salizzada San Giovanni Crisostomo
Ⓦ savevenice.org. Free.

Tucked into the southernmost corner of Cannaregio stands San Giovanni Crisostomo (John the Golden-Mouthed), named after the famously eloquent Archbishop of Constantinople. An intimate church with a compact Greek-cross plan, it was possibly the last project of Mauro Codussi, and was built between 1497 and 1504.

It possesses two outstanding altarpieces: in the chapel to the right hangs one of the last works by **Giovanni Bellini**, *SS Jerome, Christopher and Louis of Toulouse*, painted in 1513 when the artist was in his eighties; and on the high altar, **Sebastiano del Piombo**'s *St John Chrysostom with SS John the Baptist, Liberale, Mary Magdalen, Agnes and Catherine*, painted in 1509–11.

Teatro Malibran

MAP P.76, POCKET MAP G11–12
Campiello del Teatro Ⓦ teatrolafenice.it.

Behind San Giovanni Crisostomo stands the Teatro Malibran, which opened in the seventeenth century, was rebuilt in the 1790s, and soon after renamed in honour of the great soprano **Maria Malibran** (1808–36), who saved the theatre from bankruptcy by giving a fund-raising recital here. The less glamorous little sister of La Fenice, the Malibran came into its own when La Fenice was destroyed by fire in 1996, and a major restoration followed – including the installation of a massive basin to collect water during floods. The Byzantine arches on the facade of the theatre are said to have once been part of the house of **Marco Polo**'s family, who probably lived in the place overlooking the canal at the back of the Malibran, visible from the Ponte Marco Polo. Polo's tales of his experiences in the empire of Kublai Khan were treated with incredulity when he returned to Venice in 1295. His habit of talking in superlatives earned him the nickname *Il Milione* (The Million). The nickname is preserved by the adjoining **Corte Prima del Milion** and **Corte Seconda del Milion**.

Santa Maria dei Miracoli

MAP P.76, POCKET MAP G11
Campiello di Miracoli Ⓦ chorusvenezia.org.
Charge.

A hop north of the Teatro Malibran stands the exquisite marble-clad church of Santa Maria dei Miracoli, usually known simply by the last word of its name. It was built in 1481–89 to house an image of the Madonna that was credited with the revival of a man who'd spent half an hour at the bottom of the Giudecca canal, and of a woman left for dead after being stabbed. Financed by gifts left at the painting's nearby shrine, the church was most likely designed by **Pietro Lombardo**; certainly he and his two sons Tullio and Antonio oversaw the construction, and the three of them executed much of the exquisite carving both inside and out.

The marble-lined **interior** contains some of the most intricate decorative sculpture to be seen in Venice. The *Annunciation* and half-length figures of two saints on the balustrade at the altar end are thought to be by Tullio; nobody is sure which members of the family created the rest of the carvings in this part of the church, though it's likely that Antonio was responsible for the children's heads at the base of the chancel arch and the adjacent siren figures. At the opposite end of the church, the columns below the nuns' choir are covered with extraordinary filigree stonework, featuring tiny birds with legs as thin as cocktail sticks. The miracle-working Madonna still occupies the altar, while overhead a sequence of fifty saints and prophets, painted in 1528 by Pier Pennacchi, is set into the Miracoli's unusual panelled ceiling.

The Gesuiti

MAP P.76, POCKET MAP G3–H3
Salizada dei Spechieri ☎ 041 528 6579.

The major monument in the northeastern corner of Cannaregio is **Santa Maria Assunta**, commonly known simply as the Gesuiti. Built for the Jesuits in 1714–29, six decades after the foundation here of their first monastery in Venice, the church was clearly planned to make an impression on a city that was habitually mistrustful of the order's close relationship with the papacy. Although the disproportionately huge facade clearly wasn't the work of a weekend, most of the effort went into the stupefying **interior**, where green and white marble covers every wall and stone is carved to resemble swags of damask. The only painting to seek out is the *Martyrdom of St Lawrence* on the first altar on the left, showing the saint being grilled to death, painted by **Titian** in 1558.

Oratorio dei Crociferi

MAP P.76, POCKET MAP G3
Campo de Gesuiti ⓦ vistvenezia.eu. Free.

Almost opposite the Gesuiti is the Oratorio dei Crociferi, the remnant of a convent complex founded in the twelfth century by the crusading religious order known as the Crociferi or the Bearers of the Cross. Part of the complex was given over to a hospice for poor women. (By the late sixteenth century Venice had around one hundred such institutions for the penniless.) In return for free meals and accommodation, these women were required to help in the maintenance of the convent and to pray each morning in the oratory, which in the 1580s was decorated by **Palma il Giovane** with a cycle of *Scenes from the History of the Order of the Crociferi*. Restored

in the 1980s, the paintings show Palma's technique at its subtlest, and the richness of the colours is a good advertisement for modern cleaning techniques.

Fondamente Nove

MAP P.76, POCKET MAP G2–J4

The long waterfront to the north of the Gesuiti, Fondamente Nove (or Nuove), is the chief departure point for **vaporetti** to San Michele, Murano and the northern lagoon. On a clear day you can see as far as the distant island of Burano, with the startling sight of the snowy Dolomite peaks on the horizon.

Being relatively new, you'll find that this waterfront isn't solidly lined with historic buildings like its counterparts in the south of the city, the Záttere and the Riva degli Schiavone. The one house of interest along this stretch is the **Palazzo Donà delle Rose** on the corner of the Rio dei Gesuiti. Architecturally the palace is an oddity, as the main axis of its interior runs parallel to the water instead of at ninety degrees; the cornerstone was laid in 1610 by Doge Leonardo Donà, who died two years later from apoplexy after an argument with his brother about the layout of the house.

Interior view inside the Gesuiti

Shops

Atelier Leonardo

MAP P.76, POCKET MAP E3
Rio Terà San Leonardo 1703 Cannaregio
Ⓦ atelierleonardovenezia.com.

From the fourteenth century to
the early 1900s, Venetian glass
beads, known as trade beads,
were specifically designed to be
sold to African traders. Using
colours known to be significant
to different tribes, the oldest are
collectors' items. Designer Daniela
Furlan designs unique jewllery
using antique trade beads.

Despar

MAP P.76, POCKET MAP E2
Campiello de l'Anconeta 1939 Ⓦ despar.it.

Surely a contender for Europe's
most beautiful supermarket –
housed in the former Teatro Italia,
an Art Nouveau-Neo Gothic
fusion saved from decay by the
supermarket chain with a 2.5
million euro investment. Frescoes
look down on the aisles and the deli
counter occupies the former stage.

Seafood at *Anice Stellato*

Vineria Enoteca da Tellero

MAP P.76, POCKET MAP F10
Rio Terà SS. Apostoli, 4656 Castello.

Wine shop where the focus is on
vino sfuso, wine straight from the
barrel sold by the litre. Locals come
loaded with empty bottles, but if
you don't have them, new ones can
be bought for 40c. Wines start at
€2.50 a litre. Excellent selection of
(bottled) prosecco as well.

Restaurants

Ai Promessi Sposi

MAP P.76, POCKET MAP F11
Calle dell'Oca 4367 ☏ 041 241 2747.

This moderately priced and cosy
little *osteria* specializes in traditional
fish recipes, rare-breed Fassona
beef, and seasonally changing
dishes such as bigoli with duck
ragout or peas, asparagus and
artichoke. €€

Alla Fontana

MAP P.76, POCKET MAP D2
Fondamenta di Cannaregio 1102
Ⓦ trattoriaallafontana.business.site.

Once primarily a bar, *Alla Fontana* has transformed itself into an extremely good trattoria, offering a small and ever-changing menu ranging from *pasta allo scoglio* (seafood pasta) and *pasta fresca al nero di sepia* (hand-made pasta with squid ink) to fish of the day or a slow-cooked lamb shank. €€€

Alla Vedova

MAP P.76, POCKET MAP E10
Calle del Pistor 3912 ☏ 041 528 5324.
Located in an alley directly opposite the one leading to the Ca' d'Oro, this long-established little restaurant is fronted by a bar offering a mouthwatering selection of *cicheti* and wines along with excellent simple pasta dishes (try spaghetti with scampi) and hearty mains served with slabs of polenta. It's one of the best-value places in town, so if you want to sit down reservations are a good idea. No coffee or desserts. €

Anice Stellato

MAP P.76, POCKET MAP E2
Fondamenta della Sensa 3272
Ⓦ osterianicestellato.com.
Popular with Venetians for its inventive, delicious and beautifully presented food and unfussy atmosphere. Situated by one of the northernmost Cannaregio canals, it has the advantage of being rather too remote for most tourists. If you can't get a table – it's frequently booked solid – at least drop by for a glass of natural wine and some excellent *cicheti* at the bar. €€€

Da Rioba

MAP P.76, POCKET MAP F2
Fondamenta della Misericordia 2553
Ⓦ darioba.com.
This smartly austere *osteria* is another excellent northern Cannaregio restaurant; *Da Rioba* is often full to bursting, especially in summer, when tables are set beside the canal – but the atmosphere is always relaxed. Unusual dishes such as reginette pasta with guinea fowl ragù and dried plums or cappellacci

with fossa cheese, potatoes, nettle and almonds sit alongside simply grilled or baked fish and meat with innovative accompaniments – mackerel with Swiss chard olives, lemongrass and fennel, turbot with carrots and ginger cream. €€€

Gam Gam

MAP P.76, POCKET MAP D2
Calle del Ghetto Vecchio 1122 Cannaregio
Ⓦ gamgamkosher.com.
Inexpensive and much-loved Kosher restaurant famous for its matzo ball soup, gefilte fish and latkes. It also does take-away falafel and the like from the little place across the street. €

Hostaria Bacanera

MAP P.76, POCKET MAP G11
Campiello de la Cason, 4506 Cannaregio
Ⓦ bacanera.it.
Refined restaurant on a quiet campiello with an atmosphere and design that deftly translates the Venice of once upon a time into a contemporary key. Expect faultless service, and delicious versions of traditional dishes made with meticulously sourced ingredients. €€€

Marcianino

MAP P.76, POCKET MAP E2
Rio Terà Farsetti 2690A Cannaregio
☏ 041 476 7531.
Dedicated to reviving and supporting the vegetable growers of the island of Sant'Erasmo, *Marcianino* always has some good vegetable dishes – pasta e fagioli or a simple pumpkin soup – along with local fish and carefully sourced Tuscan Casentino pork and Chianina beef. Seats outside by the canal, acqua alta permitting. €€

Ostaria Santa Fosca

MAP P.76, POCKET MAP F3
Campo Santa Fosca 2321, Cannaregio
Ⓦ osteriasantafosca.com.
Although only just off the main walking route through Cannaregio to the station, this little place set

Despar supermarket, former Teatro Italia

right on a canal is perfect for a quiet aperitivo or more. Daily specials such as pasta and fagioli or *orata* (bass) baked with potatoes. Popular with Venetian regulars as well as eagle-eyed tourists. €€

Pontini

MAP P.76, POCKET MAP D3
Fondamenta Pescheria 1268
☎ 041 714123.
From outside, this looks like any number of ordinary Venetian trattoria-bars, but *Pontini* is far from ordinary: the set-priced menu consists of hearty Venetian *osteria* fare, and both the quality of the food and cheeriness of service is far better than in most touristy places. €

Vini da Gigio

MAP P.76, POCKET MAP E10
Fondamenta S. Felice 3628a ⓦ vinidagigio.it.
This family-run restaurant has made a name for its authentic, meticulously cooked renditions of Classical Venetian fare, along with more inventive dishes (risotto with pumpkin, scampi and ginger, tagliolini with spider crab, and even smoked spaghetti with carbonara). €€

Bars, cafés and gelaterie

Al Parlamento

MAP P.76, POCKET MAP C2
Fondamenta Savorgnan 511
ⓦ alparlamento.it.
This spacious and friendly bar has pale wood furnishings and lengths of rope slung across the ceiling to impart a touch of minimalist cool. There are tables outside by the canal as well. Good snacks and cocktails, and occasional live music too. €€

Bacaro al Gelato

MAP P.76, POCKET MAP F2
Fondamenta de la Misericordia, 2499
☎ 347 050 7737.
On-trend flavours made of rigorously sourced ingredients to accompany a stroll along the coolest canal in Venice – pistachio with Venezuelan chocolate, and caramel with Himalayan salt can both be vouched for. €

Combo Bacaro

MAP P.76, POCKET MAP G3
Ex Convento dei Crociferi, Campo dei Gesuiti ⓦ thisiscombo.com.
Contemporary bacaro belonging to the Combo hostel, serving superior cicheti – on toasted bread or polenta – ranging from polenta with tuna and smoked salmon to *bruschette* with brie, orange marmalade and fresh berries. There are also skewers of grilled prawns and oysters. Sit outside on the Campo and watch life stroll by. €

Dolceamaro

MAP P.76, POCKET MAP G11
Campiello San Canzian 6051 Castello
☎ 041 523 8708.
Upmarket enoteca, café and cioccolateria on a pretty square near Santa Maria dei Miracoli run by a sommelier, serving not only wine, coffee and hot chocolate, but spritzes and cocktails made with bitters and vermouths from the

iconic Poli Distillery. All manner of hand-made chocolate goodies to take away. €

Sulla Luna

MAP P.76, POCKET MAP F2
Fondamenta de la Misericordia 2535
Ⓦ sullalunavenezia.it.

Bookshop and bistrot that makes a good choice for a light, healthy lunch. Plenty of vegan options, along with cheese plates like ricotta with confit tomatoes and salad or burratina affumicata with puntarella, olives and salad. Tables right by the canal. €€

Torrefazione e Cannaregio

MAP P.76, POCKET MAP E2
Fondamenta dei Ormesini 2804
Ⓦ torrefazionecannaregio.it.

Venice was one of the first cities in Europe to import coffee beans, and coffee roasting, or *torrefazione*, is a venerable Venetian tradition. This little company has been roasting beans in Cannaregio since 1930, but there's nothing old-fashioned about its café – with its exposed bricks, upcycled wood and copious coffee sacks, this is one of the hippest and busiest cafes in town. Come early if you want there to be any cornetti left. Closes at around 4pm. €

Un Mondo di Vino

MAP P.76, POCKET MAP G11
Salizzada San Canciano 5984a
Ⓦ bacarounmondodivino.it.

Occupying a marble-fronted old butcher's shop, this brilliant little *bácaro* has rapidly built up a great reputation for its fantastic array of *cicheti*, its choice selection of wines, and the warmth of its staff. €

Volpe

MAP P.76, POCKET MAP D2
Calle del Ghetto Vecchio Cannaregio, 1143
☎ 041 715 178.

Traditional Ghetto bakery specialising in Kosher sweet goodies such as bisse, snake-shaped biscuits, impade, pastries stuffed with almond paste and azzime dolce, unleavened cookies. €

Classical music

Teatro Malibran

MAP P.76, POCKET MAP G11–12
Corte Milion 5873 Ⓦ teatrolafenice.it.

Along with the Fenice, this is the city's main venue for big-name classical concerts, opera (and occasional jazz/rock). Tickets can be bought on the night at the box office or from the same outlets as the Fenice (see page 47).

The Teatro Malibran at night

Central Castello

Bordering San Marco on one side and spreading across the city from Cannaregio in the west to the housing estates of Sant'Elena in the east, Castello is so unwieldy a *sestiere* that we've cut it in two for the purposes of this guide – this chapter starts off at its western border and stops in the east at a line drawn north from the landmark Pietà church. Castello's central building is the immense Gothic church of Santi Giovanni e Paolo (or Zanipolo), the pantheon of Venice's doges. The museums lie in the southern zone – the Querini-Stampalia picture collection, the museum at San Giorgio dei Greci, and the Museo Diocesano's sacred art collection. This southern area's dominant building is the majestic San Zaccaria, right by the southern waterfront and Venice's main promenade, the Riva degli Schiavoni.

Santi Giovanni e Paolo

MAP P.88, POCKET MAP H11
Campo SS Giovanni e Paolo
Ⓦ santigiovanniepaolo.it. Charge.

Like the Frari, the massive Gothic brick edifice of Santi Giovanni e Paolo – slurred by the Venetian dialect into **San Zanipolo** – was built for one of the mendicant orders, whose social mission (preaching to and tending the sick and the poor) required a lot of space for their congregation. The first church built on this site was begun in 1246 after **Doge Giacomo Tiepolo** (d.1249) was inspired by a dream to donate the land to the Dominicans. Tiepolo's simple sarcophagus is outside, on the left of the door, next to that of his son Doge Lorenzo Tiepolo (d.1275); the cavernous interior – approximately 90m long, 38m wide at the transepts, 33m high in the centre – houses the tombs of some 25 other doges.

Most of the **entrance wall** is given over to the glorification of the Mocenigo family, with three monuments to fifteenth-century doges from this dynasty. But the finest funerary monuments are in the **chancel**, where Doge Michele

Morosini, who ruled for just four months before dying of plague in 1382, is buried in the tomb at the front on the right, a work which to Ruskin's eyes showed "the exactly intermediate condition of feeling between the pure calmness of early Christianity, and the boastful pomp of the Renaissance faithlessness". Full-blown Renaissance pomp is represented by the **tomb of Doge Andrea Vendramin** (d.1478), diagonally opposite, while one of the earliest examples of Renaissance style in Venice – Pietro Lombardo's **tomb for Doge Pasquale Malipiero** (d.1462) – is in the left aisle, to the left of the sacristy. (The sacristy itself contains an excellent painting, Alvise Vivarini's *Christ Carrying the Cross*.) The Lombardo family were also responsible for the tombs of Doge Giovanni Mocenigo and Doge Pietro Mocenigo, to the right and left of the main door. Close by, the second altar of the right aisle is adorned by one of Zanipolo's finest paintings, **Giovanni Bellini**'s *SS Vincent Ferrer, Christopher and Sebastian*.

At the top of the right aisle, Giambattista Piazzetta's *St Dominic in Glory* covers the vault of the

Cappella di San Domenico, alongside which is a tiny shrine containing a relic of St Catherine of Siena. She died in 1380 and her body promptly entered the relic market – most of it is in Rome, but her head is in Siena, one foot is here, and lesser relics are scattered about Italy. Round the corner, in the south transept, two other superb paintings hang close together: a *Coronation of the Virgin* attributed to Cima da Conegliano and Giovanni Martini da Udine, and Lorenzo Lotto's *St Antonine* (1542).

And don't miss the **Cappella del Rosario**, at the end of the north transept. In 1867 a fire destroyed its paintings by Tintoretto, as well as Giovanni Bellini's *Madonna* and Titian's *Martyrdom of St Peter*, San Zanipolo's two most celebrated paintings. A lengthy restoration made use of surviving fragments and installed other pieces such as Veronese's ceiling panels and an *Adoration* on the left of the door.

The Colleoni monument

MAP P.88, POCKET MAP H11
Campo SS Giovanni e Paolo.

When he died in 1475, the mercenary captain **Bartolomeo Colleoni** left a legacy of some seven hundred thousand ducats to the Venetian state. But there was a snag: the Signoria could have the money only if an **equestrian monument** to him were erected in the square before San Marco – an unthinkable proposition to Venice's rulers, with their cult of anonymity. The problem was circumvented with a fine piece of disingenuousness, by which Colleoni's will was taken to permit the raising of the statue before the Scuola di San Marco, rather than the Basilica. **Andrea Verrocchio**'s statue wasn't finally unveiled until 1496, but the wait was certainly worth it: this idealized image of steely masculinity is one of the masterpieces of Renaissance sculpture.

The Scuola Grande di San Marco

MAP P.88, POCKET MAP H11
Ⓦ scuolagrandesanmarco.it. Charge.

Colleoni's backdrop, the Scuola Grande di San Marco, now provides a sumptuous facade and foyer for Venice's hospital. The facade was started by Pietro Lombardo and Giovanni Buora in 1487, half a century after the *scuola* moved here from its original home in the Santa Croce *sestiere*, and was finished in 1495 by Mauro Codussi. Taken as a whole, the trompe l'oeil arches by Tullio and Antonio Lombardo might not quite create the intended illusion, but they are nonetheless charming.

Inside, the entrance hall was designed by Mauro Codussi, who also designed the staircase that leads up to the Sala Capitolare, whose spectacular golden ceiling hangs over a collection of medical instruments and books. The Tintoretto paintings that used to adorn the walls are now in the Accademia and Milan's Brera, but two works by Tintoretto and his son are still in place. The adjacent Sala dell'Albergo,

Santi Giovanni e Paolo

also stripped of its pictures by Gentile and Giovanni Bellini, among others, now has amazingly accurate digital reproductions in their place. Next door, the Scuola di Santa Maria della Pace is now home to a collection of specimens of anatomical pathology and a reconstruction of an old pharmacy.

The Ospedaletto

MAP P.88, POCKET MAP J4
Barbaria delle Tole 6691
Ⓦ gioiellinascostidivenezia.it. Charge.
Another hospital block is attached to Longhena's church of the Ospedaletto, which stands immediately to the east of Zanipolo. Known more properly as **Santa Maria dei Derelitti**, the Ospedaletto was founded in 1528 to provide care for the desperate peasants who were forced by famine to flee the mainland that year. The church itself, with its leering giants' heads and over-ripe

decorations, drew Ruskin's wrath, who called it "the most monstrous" building in the city.

The much less extravagant **interior** has a series of eighteenth-century paintings high on the walls above the arches, one of which – *The Sacrifice of Isaac* – is an early Giambattista Tiepolo (fourth on the right). The adjoining **music room**, frescoed in the eighteenth century, is still used for concerts. At other times, the only way to see inside the Ospedaletto is by booking a private tour – details are on the website.

Santa Maria Formosa

MAP P.88, POCKET MAP H12–13
Campo Santa Maria Formosa
Ⓦ chorusvenezia.org. Charge.
The church of **Santa Maria Formosa**, which occupies one of the city's largest and most attractive squares, was founded in the seventh century by San Magno,

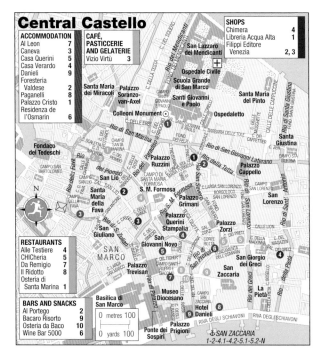

Central Castello

ACCOMMODATION	
Al Leon	7
Caneva	3
Casa Querini	3
Casa Verardo	4
Danieli	9
Foresteria Valdese	
Paganelli	8
Palazzo Cristo	1
Residenza de l'Osmarin	6

CAFÉ, PASTICCERIE AND GELATERIE	
Vizio Virtù	3

SHOPS	
Chimera	4
Libreria Acqua Alta	1
Filippi Editore	
Venezia	2, 3

RESTAURANTS	
Alle Testiere	4
CHICheria	5
Da Remigio	7
Il Ridotto	8
Osteria di Santa Marina	1

BARS AND SNACKS	
Al Portego	2
Bacaro Risorto	9
Osteria da Baco	5
Wine Bar 5000	6

0 metres 100
0 yards 100

SAN ZACCARIA
1-2-4.1-4.2-5.1-5.2-N

Bishop of Oderzo, who was guided by a dream in which he saw the Madonna *formosa* – a word which most closely translates as buxom and beautiful. Outside, the most unusual feature is the face at the base of the campanile: it's been argued that it is both a talisman against the evil eye and a piece of clinical realism, portraying a man with a disorder of the sort that disfigured Joseph Merrick, the so-called Elephant Man. The church contains two good paintings. Entering from the west side, the first one you'll see is Bartolomeo Vivarini's triptych of *The Madonna of the Misericordia* (1473), in a nave chapel on the right-hand side of the church. Nearby, closer to the main altar, is Palma il Vecchio's *St Barbara* (1522–24), praised by George Eliot as "an almost unique presentation of a hero-woman".

North facade of Santa Maria Formosa

Palazzo Grimani

MAP P.88, POCKET MAP H13
Ruga Giuffa Ⓦ palazzogrimani.org. Charge.

South of Santa Maria Formosa, if you turn first left off Ruga Giuffa you'll be confronted by the gargantuan sixteenth-century **Palazzo Grimani**, once owned by the branch of the Grimani family whose collection of antiquities became the basis of the Museo Archeologico. The neo-Roman interior, featuring some of the most spectacular rooms in the city, has been beautifully restored and furnished with a miscellany of *objets d'art*. Special exhibitions are often held here too.

Santa Maria della Fava

MAP P.88, POCKET MAP G13
Campo della Fava Ⓣ 041 5224601. Free.

Between Santa Maria Formosa and the Rialto stands the church of **Santa Maria della Fava** (or Santa Maria della Consolazione), whose peculiar name derives from a sweet cake – a bit like a hard meringue made of almonds, sugar and egg white – called a *fava* (bean), once

an All Souls' Day speciality of a local baker and still a seasonal treat. On the first altar on the right stands Giambattista Tiepolo's early *Education of the Virgin* (1732); on the other side of the church there's *The Madonna and St Philip Neri*, painted five years earlier by the influential Giambattista Piazzetta.

Palazzo Querini-Stampalia

MAP P.88, POCKET MAP H13
Campo di Santa Maria Formosa
Ⓦ querinistampalia.it. Charge.

On the south side of Campo di Santa Maria Formosa, a footbridge over a narrow canal leads into the **Palazzo Querini-Stampalia**, home of the Pinacoteca Querini-Stampalia. Although there is a batch of Renaissance pieces – such as Palma il Vecchio's marriage portraits of Francesco Querini and Paola Priuli Querini (for whom the palace was built), and **Giovanni Bellini**'s *Presentation in the Temple* – the general tone of the collection is set by the culture of eighteenth-century Venice, a period to which much of the palace's decor belongs. The winningly inept pieces by **Gabriel Bella** form a comprehensive record of Venetian street life, while life within the walls of the palazzo is perhaps best captured in the exquisite pale pink dining room, its table set for a banquet with Sèvres porcelain and Murano glass. One other notable aspect of this museum is that its basement rooms (where good contemporary art shows are often held) a play of water with marble conceived by Carlo Scarpa, who also designed the entrance bridge and the garden – an ensemble that constitutes one of Venice's extremely rare examples of first-class modern architecture as well as providing a wonderful setting for the museum's café.

San Zaccaria

MAP P.88, POCKET MAP J6
Campo San Zaccaria Ⓦ chorusvenezia.org. Charge.

Elegant **Campo San Zaccaria** is a spot with a bloody past. In 864 **Doge Pietro Tradonico** was murdered in the campo as he returned from vespers, and in 1172 **Doge Vitale Michiel II**, having not only blundered in peace negotiations with the Byzantine empire but also brought the plague back with him from Constantinople, was murdered as he fled for the sanctuary of San Zaccaria.

Founded in the ninth century as a shrine for the body of Zaccharias, father of John the Baptist, the church of San Zaccaria had already been rebuilt several times when, in 1444, Antonio Gambello embarked on a rebuilding that was concluded some seventy years later by Mauro Codussi, who took over the facade from the first storey upwards. The end result is a distinctively Venetian mixture of Gothic and Renaissance styles.

The interior's notable architectural feature is its **ambulatory**: unique in Venice, it might have been built to accommodate the annual ritual of the doges' Easter Sunday visit. Nearly every inch of wall surface is hung with seventeenth- and eighteenth-century paintings, all of them outshone by Giovanni **Bellini**'s *Madonna and Four Saints* (1505), on the second altar on the left. The Cappella di Sant'Atanasio and Cappella di San Tarasio (off the right aisle) have wonderful altarpieces by Antonio Vivarini

View of the Palazzo Grimani from the Grand Canal

and Giovanni d'Alemagna (all 1443). Steps descend to the almost perpetually waterlogged ninth-century crypt, the burial place of eight early doges.

The Riva degli Schiavoni

MAP P.88, POCKET MAP H15/H6–K6

The broad Riva degli Schiavoni, stretching from the edge of the Palazzo Ducale almost as far as the Arsenale canal, is usually thronged with promenading tourists and passengers hurrying to and from its vaporetto stops, threading through the souvenir stalls and past the wares of the illicit street vendors. The Riva has long been one of Venice's smart addresses. Petrarch and his daughter lived at no. 4145 in 1362–67, and Henry James stayed at no. 4161, battling against constant distractions to finish *The Portrait of a Lady*. George Sand, Charles Dickens, Proust, Wagner and the ever-present Ruskin all checked in at the *Hotel Danieli* (see page 131).

La Pietà

MAP P.88, POCKET MAP J6

Riva degli Schiavoni ☎ 041 522 2171. Charge.

The main eyecatcher on the Riva is the white facade of **Santa Maria della Visitazione**, known as La Pietà. **Vivaldi** wrote many of his finest pieces for the orphanage attached to the church, where he worked as violin-master (1704–18) and choirmaster (1735–38). During Vivaldi's second term, Massari won a competition to rebuild the church, and it's probable that the composer advised him on acoustics. Building began in 1745 (after Vivaldi's death), and when the interior was completed in 1760 it was regarded more as a concert hall than a church. The white and gold interior is crowned by a superb ceiling painting, *The Glory of Paradise* by Giambattista Tiepolo, who also painted the ceiling panel above the altar. The Pietà's in-house orchestra

Monument on the Riva degli Schiavoni

plays Vivaldi here two or three times a week, with the *Four Seasons* always on the bill.

The Greek quarter

MAP P.88, POCKET MAP J5

Salizzada dei Greci ⓦ istitutoellenico.org. Charge.

To the north of La Pietà, the campanile of **San Giorgio dei Greci** tilts hazardously canalwards. The **Greek** presence in Venice was strong from the eleventh century and became stronger still after the Turkish seizure of Constantinople. Built a century later, the church has Orthodox architectural elements including a *matroneo* (women's gallery) and an iconostasis that completely cuts off the high altar. The icons on the screen include a few Byzantine pieces dating back as far as the twelfth century.

The adjacent Scuola di San Nicolò dei Greci now houses the **Museo di Dipinti Sacri Bizantini**, a collection of predominantly fifteenth- to eighteenth-century icons, many of them by the *Madoneri*, the school of Greek and Cretan artists working in Venice in that period.

Shops

Chimera

MAP P.88, POCKET MAP J5
Salizzada dei Greci 3459 ☎ 349 876 4981.
Hand-made ceramics (the oven
is in the shop), enamel jewellery,
brocade bags and watercolour
prints all at very reasonable prices.

Libreria Acqua Alta

MAP P.88, POCKET MAP H12
Calle Lunga Santa Maria Formosa 5176b
ⓦ facebook.com/libreriaacquaalta.
Luigi Frizzi's labyrinthine bookshop
is like no other, with thousands
of books – nearly all secondhand,
and nearly all Italian – stacked on
every available surface, with some
displayed in bathtubs and even in a
gondola, to protect them from high
tides (the back door opens directly
into the water). There's even a
staircase built from water-damaged
hardbacks.

Filippi Editore Venezia

MAP P.88, POCKET MAP G13
Caselleria 5284 & Calle del Paradiso 5763
ⓦ libreriaeditricefilippi.com.
The family-run Filippi business
produces a vast range of Venice-
related facsimile editions, including
Francesco Sansovino's sixteenth-
century guide to the city (the first
city guide ever published), and sells
an amazing stock of books about
Venice in its two shops.

Café, pasticcerie and gelaterie

Vizio Virtù

MAP P.88, POCKET MAP G12
Calle del Forner/Calle della Malvasia 5988
ⓦ viziovirtu.com.
Chocolate specialist where you
can taste hot chocolate made to a
recipe of 1750 discovered in the
Casa Goldoni – the chocolate
is flavoured with cinnamon,
cardamon, chilli, vanilla and ginger
and infused with water or hot milk.
Hand-made chocolates to die for
as well – check out the huge range
of chocolate dipped candied fruits
including a surprisingly delicious
candied black olive. €

Restaurants

Alle Testiere

MAP P.88, POCKET MAP H13
Calle Mondo Nuovo 5801
ⓦ osterialletestiere.it.
Very small, very special and rather
pricey fish and seafood restaurant
in the alley on the other side of the
canal from the front of Santa Maria
Formosa, with an ever-changing
menu and a superb wine selection.
Lagoon-caught fish and seafood
are a speciality – look out for little
local langoustines served raw,
little gnocchi with tiny calamari
and cinnamon, or lagoon fish and
seafood grilled on the barbeque.
In the evening there are sittings at
7pm and 9.30pm, to handle the
demand – booking via the website
is obligatory. 7pm slots sell out
months in advance. €€€€

CHICheria

MAP P.88, POCKET MAP J5
Fondamenta de L'Osmarin 4984
ⓦ chiceria.it.
Opened in August 2023, this
elegant, intimate and understated
restaurant is becoming known for its
inventive and sophisticated cuisine.
The stand-out dish is spaghetti in a
prawn bisque with confit tomatoes
served on a bed of wafer-thin raw
prawn which is cooked by the heat
of the pasta. €€€€

Da Remigio

MAP P.88, POCKET MAP J5
Salizzada dei Greci 3416
ⓦ facebook.com/TrattoriaDaRemigio.
Well-established trattoria, serving
excellent fish dishes – a fine place
for local razor clams with garlic
and black pepper, hand-made
pasta with prawns, courgettes

and asparagus or roast scorfanetti (little scorpion fish). The wine list is outstanding too. Be sure to book – the locals (and increasingly tourists) pack this place every night. €€€

Il Ridotto

MAP P.88, POCKET MAP H14
Campo Santi Filippo e Giacomo 4509
Ⓦ ilridotto.com.
Founded in 2006 this is one of the best-regarded restaurants within a short radius of the Piazza. If you want to splash out, opt for either a la carte or one of the 5- or 7-course tasting menus, but if you are looking to eat exceptionally well without breaking the bank, there are some very fair-priced lunchtime deals. €€€€

Osteria di Santa Marina

MAP P.88, POCKET MAP G12
Campo Santa Marina 5911
Ⓦ osteriadisantamarina.com.
Despite the traditional wooden interior, this is a very slick and impressive modern operation offering imaginative variants on Venetian maritime standards on the set menus, and sheer imagination a la carte – cauliflower risotto with an egg yolk marinated in green tea, caviar and sea urchin gives some idea. The wine list is impressive too. €€€

Bars and snacks

Al Portego

MAP P.88, POCKET MAP G12
Calle Malvasia 6015
Ⓦ osteriaalportego.org.
In the middle of the day this bar is crammed with customers eating glistening fresh *cicheti* – look out for artichoke, ricotta and almond, or pumpkin, radicchio and ricotta – and in the evening there's often a queue for a place at one of the tiny tables, where some well-prepared basics (pasta, risotto, etc) are served. No reservations are taken. €

Libreria Acqua Alta

Bacaro Risorto

MAP P.88, POCKET MAP J6
Campo San Provolo 4700 ☎ 340 301 7047.
Friendly place serving a superior array of traditional cicheti using locally sourced fish and meat. Some good veggie options too, such as roast pumpkin with scamorza cheese. Carnivores flock here for the daily specials, many of them offal-based. €

Osteria da Baco

MAP P.88, POCKET MAP H14
Calle delle Rasse 4620 ☎ 041 241 1423.
Da Baco is the nearest genuine old-style *osteria* to the Piazza, with an excellent range of sandwiches and other snacks. €

Wine Bar 5000

MAP P.88, POCKET MAP J5
Fondamenta San Severo 5000
Ⓦ winebar5000.it.
Café and bar with a terrace in a tranquil canalside corner of the city. Good cocktails and superior but affordable cicheti that change every day. €

Eastern Castello

Sights are more thinly spread in the eastern section of the Castello *sestiere*, and a huge bite is taken out of the area by the dockyards of the Arsenale, yet this easternmost slab of Venice makes a refreshing and relaxing contrast to the intense concentration of sights and tourists that characterize much of the city. Streets broaden out, the glimpses of sky increase, and beyond the Arsenale, many of the residential streets and canals of Sant'Elena are lined with trees. The two focal points of the area are the Arsenale and the Biennale gardens – but few tourists wander beyond the sites. As for sights, the highlight is the Scuola di San Giorgio degli Schiavoni, with its endearing cycle of paintings by Carpaccio, and the famous lion gate of the Arsenale. And although the mainly residential area beyond the Arsenale has little to offer in the way of cultural monuments, there are some great little places to eat, while the waterfront gives spectacular panoramas of the city.

San Francesco della Vigna

MAP P.96, POCKET MAP K4
Calle S. Francesco Ⓦ facebook.com/
SanFrancescoDellaVignaVenezia. Free.
The area that lies to the **east of San Zanipolo** is not an attractive

district at first sight, but carry on east along Barbaria delle Tole for just a couple of minutes and a striking Renaissance facade blocks your way. The ground occupied by San Francesco della Vigna has

Ceiling fresco with scenes from *Apocalypse* at the San Francesco della Vigna church

a hallowed place in the mythology of Venice, as according to tradition it was around here that the angel appeared to St Mark to tell him that the lagoon islands were to be his final resting place. Begun in 1534, the present building was much modified in the course of its construction. Palladio was brought in to provide the facade, a feature that looks like something of an afterthought from the side, but which must have been stunning at the time. The **interior** has some fine works of art, notably a glowingly colourful *Madonna and Child Enthroned* by Antonio da Negroponte (right transept), marvellous sculpture by the Lombardo family in the Giustiniani chapel (left of the chancel), and a *Sacra Conversazione* by Veronese (last chapel of the left aisle). A door at the end of the transept leads to a pair of tranquil fifteenth-century cloisters, via the **Cappella Santa**, which has a *Madonna and Child* by Giovanni Bellini and assistants.

Piazza and tower at the Arsenale

The Scuola di San Giorgio degli Schiavoni

MAP P.96, POCKET MAP J5
Calle dei Furlani
Ⓦ scuoladalmatavenezia.com. Reservations via website obligatory. Charge.

Venice has two brilliant cycles of pictures by **Vittore Carpaccio**, one of the most disarming of Venetian artists – one is in the Accademia, the other in the Scuola di San Giorgio degli Schiavoni, the confraternity of Venice's Slavic community. The cycle illustrates mainly the lives of the Dalmatian patron saints – George, Tryphone and Jerome. As always with Carpaccio, what holds your attention is not so much the main event as the incidental details with which he packs the scene, such as the limb-strewn feeding-ground of St George's dragon, or the endearing little white dog in *The Vision of St Augustine* (he was writing to St Jerome when a vision told him of Jerome's death).

San Giovanni in Brágora

MAP P.96, POCKET MAP K6
Campo della Bràgora Ⓦ chorusvenezia.org. Charge.

San Giovanni in Brágora is probably best known to Venetians as the baptismal church of Antonio Vivaldi. The church is dedicated to the Baptist, and some people think that its strange suffix is a reference to a region from which some relics of the saint were once brought; others link the name to the old dialect words for mud (*brago*) and backwater (*gora*). The present structure was begun in 1475, and its best paintings were created within a quarter-century of the rebuilding: a triptych by **Bartolomeo Vivarini**, on the wall between the first and second chapels on the right; a *Resurrection* by **Alvise Vivarini**, to the left of the sacristy door; and two paintings by **Cima da Conegliano** – a *SS Helen and Constantine*, to the right of the sacristy door, and a *Baptism* on the high altar.

The Arsenale

MAP P.96, POCKET MAP K5–L6

A corruption of the Arabic *darsin'a* (house of industry), the very name of the Arsenale is indicative of the strength of Venice's links with the eastern Mediterranean, and the workers of these dockyards and factories were the foundations upon which the city's maritime supremacy rested. By the 1420s it had become the base for some 300 shipping companies, operating around 3000 vessels of 200 tons or more; at the Arsenale's zenith, around the middle of the sixteenth century, its wet and dry docks, its rope and sail factories, its ordnance depots and gunpowder mills employed a total of 16,000 men – equal to the population of a major town of the period.

There is no public access to the Arsenale, but you can inspect the magnificent **gateway** at close quarters. The first structure in Venice to employ the classical vocabulary of Renaissance architecture, it is guarded by four photogenic lions brought here from Greece: the two furthest on the right probably came from the Lion Terrace at Delos, and date from around the sixth century BC; the larger pair were stolen from Piraeus in 1687 by Francesco Morosini.

The Museo Storico Navale

MAP P.96, POCKET MAP K6–L6

Riva San Biasio Ⓦ visitmuve.it. Charge. Documenting every facet of Venice's naval history, the Museo Storico Navale is a somewhat diffuse museum, but a selective tour is an essential supplement to a walk round the Arsenale district. Models of Venetian craft and battleships – from the gondola to the 224-oar fighting galley and the last *Bucintoro* (the state ceremonial galley) – share space with miscellaneous armaments and other naval items.

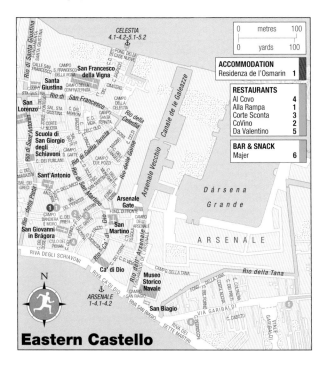

View from San Marco Canal of Via Garibaldi and the embankment at sunset

Via Garibaldi and San Pietro di Castello

MAP P.96, POCKET MAP L7

In 1808 the greater part of the canal connecting the Bacino di San Marco to the broad northeastern inlet of the Canale di San Pietro was filled in to form what is now Via Garibaldi, the widest street in the city and the social hub of the eastern district. Via Garibaldi points the way to the island of **San Pietro**, one of the first parts of central Venice to be inhabited. Nowadays this is a workaday district where the repairing of boats is the main occupation, yet it was once the ecclesiastical centre of Venice, having been the seat of the **Patriarch of Venice** until 1807. As with the Arsenale, the history of San Pietro is somewhat more interesting than what you can see. The present San Pietro di Castello (ⓦchorusvenezia.org) is a fairly charmless church, its most interesting features being the stone-clad and precarious **campanile**, and the so-called **Throne of St Peter** (in the right aisle), a marble seat made in the thirteenth century from an Arabic funeral stone cut with texts from the Koran. A late work by

Veronese, *SS John the Evangelist, Peter and Paul,* hangs by the entrance to the Cappello Lando (left aisle), where you'll find a bust of St Lorenzo Giustiniani, the first Patriarch of Venice. Giustiniani, who died in 1456, lies in the glass case within the elaborate high altar, which was designed by Longhena.

The public gardens and the Biennale site

MAP P.98, POCKET MAP M8

Stretching from Via Garibaldi to the Rio di Sant'Elena, the arc of green spaces formed by the **Giardini Garibaldi**, **Giardini Pubblici** and **Parco delle Rimembranze** provide a remedy for the claustrophobia that overtakes many visitors to Venice at some point. Largely obscured by the trees are the rather more extensive grounds belonging to the Biennale, a dormant zone except when the art and architecture shindigs are in progress (in the summer of even- and odd-numbered years respectively; see page 145). Various countries have built permanent pavilions for their Biennale representatives, forming a unique colony that features work by

View of Sant'Elena and San Pietro

Sant'Elena

MAP P.98

The island of Sant'Elena, the city's eastern limit, was greatly enlarged during the Austrian administration, partly to furnish accommodation and exercise grounds for the occupying troops. Its sole monument is Sant'Elena church, founded in the thirteenth century to house the body of St Helena, Constantine's mother. Approached between the walls of the naval college and the ramshackle home of Venice's football team, it's worth visiting for the fine **doorway**, an ensemble incorporating the **monument to Vittore Cappello**, captain-general of the republic's navy in the 1460s, showing him kneeling before St Helena. Inside the church, a chapel on the right enshrines the alleged remains of Helena, whose body is more generally believed to lie in a tomb in Rome's church of Santa Maria in Aracoeli.

some of the great names of modern architecture and design, such as Alvar Aalto, Gerrit Thomas Rietveld and Carlo Scarpa.

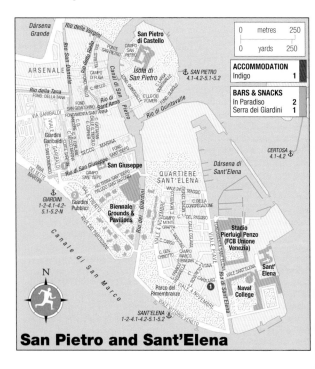

San Pietro and Sant'Elena

Restaurants

Al Covo

MAP P.96, POCKET MAP K6
Campiello della Pescaria 3968
Ⓦ ristorantealcovo.com.

Located in a backwater to the east of Campo Bandiera e Moro, *Covo* is one of Venice's foodie havens, with a consistently high reputation for scrupulous sourcing of fish and meat and growing as much of the vegetables as possible. €€€

Alla Rampa

MAP P.96, POCKET MAP K6
Salizzada S. Antonin 3607 ☏ 347 851 3908.

Shabby and totally authentic bar, has been here for half a century. Great for an inexpensive *ombra* it still serves cheap set lunches of hearty Venetian specialties such as polenta with cuttlefish for local construction workers. Prices are slightly more for anyone who has clearly not just walked off a building site. €

Corte Sconta

MAP P.96, POCKET MAP K6
Calle del Pestrin 3886 Ⓦ cortescontave.com.

In a lane to the east of San Giovanni in Brágora, this is one of Venice's finest. Expect refined dishes such as a carpaccio of swordfish with citrus fruit and tarragon, or handmade pasta with scallops and chanterelles. The antipasto set menu is great for lunch and the tasting menu is competitively priced. Booking days in advance is essential. €€€

CoVino

MAP P.96, POCKET MAP K6
Calle del Pestrin 3829 Ⓦ covinovenezia.com.

This fourteen-seat micro-restaurant is regarded by some as one of Venice's best places to eat, though others find it a little pretentious. But nobody would dispute that it's unlike anywhere else in the city, and is serious about its food. You pay a fixed price for three courses and a dessert, coffee and digestive, but there are also options to choose one, two or three courses, with dessert, coffee and digestive included. €€

Da Valentino

MAP P.96, POCKET MAP M7
Via Garibaldi 1137.

Gritty and authentic place where local workers flock for lunch. A chalkboard outside lists the day's offerings – expect the likes of sausage risotto or pasta al ragù. You won't eat cheaper anywhere in Venice. €

Bars and snacks

In Paradiso

MAP P.98, POCKET MAP M8
1260 Giardini della Biennale, Castello
Ⓦ inparadiso.net.

Located in a wisteria-festooned glasshouse on the edge of the Biennale gardens, right on the waterfront, this is a spectacular choice for an evening aperitivo. If you are with a crowd or on a mission, spritz can served by the litre. €

Majer

MAP P.96, POCKET MAP L7
Via Garibaldi 1591 Castello Ⓦ majer.it.

Branch of Venice's best chain of cafés and wine bars. This one specialises in sweet and savoury baked goodies including excellent cornetti with very good coffee, and pizza slices, sandwiches and tagliere of cold cuts accompanied by natural wine or craft beer. Plenty of tables outside. €

Serra dei Giardini

MAP P.98, POCKET MAP M7
Giardini Pubblici snc, Castello
Ⓦ serradeigiardini.org.

Café and garden centre in a beautifully restored late nineteenth century glasshouse, popular with Venetian hipsters and families. Great coffee and cakes along with organic juices. And some beautiful house plants to boot. The initiative is run by an environmental co-operative – see the website for a packed programme of events and experiences for adults and children. €

The Canal Grande

The Canal Grande is Venice's high street, and divides the city in half, with three *sestieri* to the west and three to the east. Four bridges cross the waterway – the Calatrava, plus those at the Scalzi (train station), Rialto and Accademia – but you may also find gondola traghetti crossing points. Bear in mind too that the #1 vaporetto slaloms from one bank to the other along its entire length. The Canal Grande is almost four kilometres long and varies in width between thirty and seventy metres; it is, however, surprisingly shallow, at no point much exceeding five metres. The section that follows is principally a selection of Canal Grande palaces. It's arranged as three sections, first covering the bridges, followed by the right bank (to your right as you travel down from the train station) then the left bank; surveying both banks simultaneously is possible only from a seat right at the front or the back of a vaporetto.

The bridges

The Calatrava and Scalzi bridges

MAP P.102, POCKET MAP B4 & C4

Officially known as the **Ponte della Costituzione**, but Venetians call it the **Ponte di Calatrava**, after its designer, Santiago Calatrava. Erected in 2007, the single span – an elegant arc of steel, stone and glass – is modelled on the shape of a gondola's hull.

Downstream, more or less in front of the station, lies the **Ponte**

Gondola near Rialto Bridge

Venetian palazzi

Virtually all the surviving Canal Grande palaces were built over a span of about five hundred years, and in the course of that period the **basic plan** varied very little. The typical palace has an entrance hall (the **andron**) on the ground floor, and this runs right through the building, flanked by storage rooms. Above this, there is often a mezzanine – the small rooms on this level were used as offices or, from the sixteenth century onwards, as libraries or living rooms. On the next floor – often the most extravagantly decorated – you find the **piano nobile**, the main living area, arranged as suites on each side of a central hall (**portego**), which runs, like the *andron*, from front to back. The plan of these houses can be read from the outside, where you'll usually see a cluster of large windows in the centre of the facade, between symmetrically placed side windows. Frequently there is a second *piano nobile* above the first – this generally would have been accommodation for relatives or children, though sometimes it was the main living quarters; the attic would contain servants' rooms or storage.

degli Scalzi, successor of an iron structure put up by the Austrians in 1858–60; like the one at the Accademia, it was replaced in the early 1930s to give the new steamboats sufficient clearance.

Rialto Bridge
MAP P.102, POCKET MAP F12

The famous Ponte di Rialto superseded a succession of wooden structures – one of Carpaccio's *Miracles of the True Cross*, in the Accademia, shows one of them. The decision to construct a stone bridge was taken in 1524, and eventually the job was awarded to **Antonio da Ponte**. Until 1854, when the Accademia bridge was built, this was the only point at which the Canal Grande could be crossed on foot.

Accademia Bridge
MAP P.102, POCKET MAP C16

As the larger vaporetti couldn't get under the iron Ponte dell' Accademia built by the Austrians in 1854, it was replaced in 1932 by a wooden one – a temporary measure that became permanent with the addition of a reinforcing steel substructure.

The Right Bank

Fondaco dei Turchi
MAP P.102, POCKET MAP C10

Having first passed the green-domed church of **San Simeone Piccolo** and a procession of nondescript buildings, you come to the Fondaco dei Turchi. A private house from the early thirteenth century until 1621, it was then turned over to Turkish traders, who stayed here until 1838. Though it's been over-restored, the building's towers and water-level arcade give a reasonably precise picture of what a Veneto-Byzantine palace would have looked like.

Ca' Pésaro
MAP P.102, POCKET MAP D10

A short distance beyond the church of **San Stae** stands the thickly ornamented Ca' Pésaro, bristling with diamond-shaped spikes and grotesque heads. Three houses had to be demolished to make room for this palace and its construction lasted half a century – work finished in 1703, long after the death of the architect, Baldassare Longhena.

Canal Grande

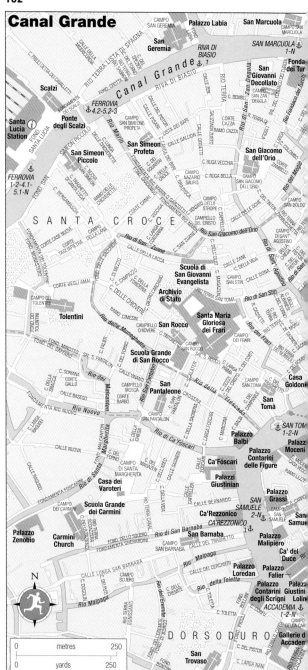

CAMPO SAN GEREMIA

Palazzo Labia

San Marcuola

CAMPO SAN MARCUOLA

San Geremia

RIVA DI BIASIO

SAN MARCUOLA 1-N

Canal Grande 1

RIVA DI BIASIO

San Giovanni Decollato

Fonda dei Tur

Scalzi

FERROVIA 4.2-5.2-3

Santa Lucia Station

Ponte degli Scalzi

San Giacomo dell'Orio

FERROVIA 1-2-4.1-5.1-N

San Simeon Piccolo

San Simeon Profeta

CAMPO NAZARIO SAURO

CAMPO SAN GIACOMO DELL'ORIO

SANTA   CROCE

Scuola di San Giovanni Evangelista

Archivio di Stato

Tolentini

San Rocco

Santa Maria Gloriosa dei Frari

CAMPO DEI FRARI

Scuola Grande di San Rocco

CAMPO SAN ROCCO

San Pantaleone

San Tomà

Casa Goldoni

Rio Nuovo

CAMPO SAN PANTALON

SAN TOMÀ 1-2-N

Palazzo Balbi

Palazzo Moceni

Ca'Fóscari

Palazzo Contarini delle Figure

CAMPO DI SANTA MARGHERITA

Palazzi Giustinian

Palazzo Grassi

Casa dei Varoteri

SAN SAMUELE 2-N

San Samue

Scuola Grande dei Carmini

Ca'Rezzonico

CA'REZZONICO 1

CAMPO SAN SAMUELE

Palazzo Zenobio

Carmini Church

San Barnaba

CAMPO SAN BARNABA

Palazzo Malipiero

Ca' del Duce

Palazzo Loredan

Palazzo Falier

Palazzo Contarini degli Scrigni

Palazzo Giustini Lolin

ACCADEMIA 1-2-N

Gallerie d Accadem

N

DORSODURO

San Trovaso

| 0 | metres | 250 |
| 0 | yards | 250 |

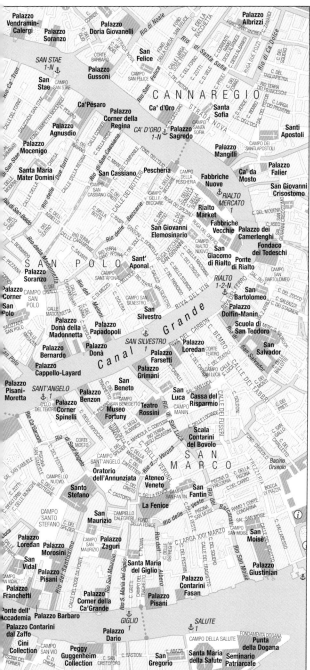

Palazzo Vendramin-Calergi

Palazzo Soranzo

C. CORRER

FOND. DELLA MISERICORDIA

Palazzo Doria Giovanelli

FOND. DELLA RACCHETTA

Palazzo Albrizzi

FOND. SANT'ANDREA

RUGA DUE POZZI

RIO di Ca' Dolce

C. DEL SALEGO

SAN STAE 1-N

San Stae

SALIZADA SAN STAE

CAMPO SAN STAE

CORTE BARBARO

STRADA NOVA

San Felice

CAMPO SAN FELICE

RIO di Santa Sofia

CANNAREGIO

Palazzo Gussoni

Ca'Pésaro

Palazzo Corner della Regina

Ca' d'Oro

CA' D'ORO 1-N

Palazzo Sagredo

Santa Sofia

Santi Apostoli

CAMPO DEI SANTI APOSTOLI

Palazzo Agnusdio

Palazzo Mocenigo

RIO delle Due Torri

Santa Maria Mater Domini

San Cassiano

Pescheria

CAMPO DELLA PESCHERIA

Palazzo Mangilli

Fabbriche Nuove

Ca' da Mosto

RIALTO MERCATO

Palazzo Falier

San Giovanni Crisostomo

Rialto Market

Palazzo dei Camerlenghi

SAN POLO

Palazzo Soranzo

Sant' Aponal

San Giovanni Elemosinario

Fabbriche Vecchie

San Giacomo di Rialto

Fondaco dei Tedeschi

Ponte di Rialto

RIALTO 1-2-N

Palazzo Corner

CAMPO SAN POLO

San Polo

San Silvestro

CAMPO SAN SILVESTRO

RIVA DEL VIN

Canal Grande

San Bartolomeo

Palazzo Dolfin-Manin

Scuola di San Teodoro

San Salvador

Palazzo Donà della Madonnetta

Palazzo Papadopoli

SAN SILVESTRO 1

Palazzo Donà

Palazzo Loredan

Palazzo Bernardo

Palazzo Cappello-Layard

Palazzo Pisani-Moretta

SANT'ANGELO

Palazzo Corner Spinelli

San Beneto

Palazzo Grimani

Palazzo Benzon

Museo Fortuny

Teatro Rossini

CAMPO MANIN

Cassa del Risparmio

Scala Contarini del Bovolo

RIO di San Luca

San Luca

Palazzo Farsetti

RIO di Verona

Oratorio dell'Annunziata

Ateneo Veneto

San Fantin

SAN MARCO

Santo Stefano

San Maurizio

La Fenice

San Fantin

San Moisè

CAMPO SANTO STEFANO

Palazzo Loredan

Palazzo Morosini

San Vidal

Palazzo Zaguri

Santa Maria del Giglio

Palazzo Contarini Fasan

Palazzo Giustinian

Palazzo Pisani

Palazzo Franchetti

Palazzo Corner della Ca'Grande

Palazzo Pisani

GIGLIO 1

Ponte dell'Accademia

Palazzo Barbaro

Palazzo Dario

SALUTE

Palazzo Contarini dal Zaffo

Cini Collection

Peggy Guggenheim Collection

San Gregorio

Santa Maria della Salute

Punta della Dogana

Seminario Patriarcale

View of Palazzo dei Camerlenghi

Palazzo Corner della Regina

MAP P.102, POCKET MAP D10–11

The next large building is the Palazzo Corner della Regina, built in 1724 on the site of the home of **Caterina Cornaro**, Queen of Cyprus, from whom the palace takes its name. It was formerly the *Monte di Pietà*, or municipal pawnshop.

Rialto market

MAP P.102, POCKET MAP E11–F12

The Rialto markets begin with the neo-Gothic fish market, the **Pescheria**, built in 1907; there's been a fish market here since the fourteenth century. The older buildings that follow it, the **Fabbriche Nuove di Rialto** and (set back from the water) the **Fabbriche Vecchie di Rialto**, are by Sansovino (1555) and Scarpagnino (1522) respectively.

Palazzo dei Camerlenghi

MAP P.102, POCKET MAP F12

The large building at the base of the Rialto bridge is the Palazzo dei Camerlenghi (c.1525), the former chambers of the Venetian exchequer.

Palazzo Balbi

MAP P.102, POCKET MAP B14

The Palazzo Balbi, on the Volta del Canal, is a proto-Baroque design executed in the 1580s to plans by Alessandro Vittoria, whose sculptures feature in many Venetian churches. Nicolò Balbi is reputed to have moored a boat alongside the building site so that he could watch the work progressing on his house – and died of the chill he consequently caught.

Ca' Fóscari

MAP P.102, POCKET MAP B14

On the opposite bank stands the Ca' Fóscari (c.1435). The largest private house in Venice at the time of its construction, it was the home of Doge Francesco Fóscari, whose extraordinarily long term of office (34 years) came to an end with his forced resignation. Venice's university now owns the building.

The Palazzi Giustinian

MAP P.102, POCKET MAP B14

The Palazzi Giustinian are a pair of palaces built in the mid-fifteenth century for two brothers who wanted attached but self-contained houses. One of the palazzi was **Wagner**'s home for a while.

Ca' Rezzonico

MAP P.102, POCKET MAP B15

Longhena's gargantuan Ca' Rezzonico was begun in 1667 as a commission from the Bon family, but they were obliged to sell the still unfinished palace to the Rezzonico, a family of stupendously wealthy Genoese bankers. Among its subsequent owners was Pen Browning, whose father, the poet, Robert, died here in 1889. See page 57.

Palazzo Venier dei Leoni

MAP P.102, POCKET MAP D16

The Venier family, one of Venice's great dynasties, had their main base just beyond the Campo San Vio. In 1759 the Veniers began rebuilding their home, but the Palazzo Venier dei Leoni, which would have been the largest palace on the canal, never progressed further than the first storey – hence its alternative name, **Palazzo Nonfinito**. The stump of the building is occupied by the Guggenheim museum (see page 49).

Palazzo Dario
MAP P.102, POCKET MAP D16
The one domestic building of interest between the Guggenheim and the end of the canal is the miniature Palazzo Dario. It was built in the late 1480s, and the multicoloured marbles of the facade are characteristic of the work of the Lombardo family.

Dogana di Mare
MAP P.102, POCKET MAP F16
The focal point of this last stretch of the canal is Longhena's masterpiece, **Santa Maria della Salute**, after which comes the Dogana di Mare (Customs House), the Canal Grande's full stop, which now houses the art collection of François Pinault. See also page 50.

The Left Bank
Palazzo Labia
MAP P.102, POCKET MAP D3
The boat passes two churches, the **Scalzi** and **San Geremia**, before the first of the major palaces comes into view on the left – the Palazzo Labia. This huge house was completed c.1750, for a madly wealthy Catalan family by the name of Lasbias. The main facade stretches along the Cannaregio canal, but from the Canal Grande you can see how the side wing wraps itself round the campanile of the neighbouring church of San Geremia – such interlocking is common in Venice, to make maximum use of available space.

Palazzo Vendramin-Calergi
MAP P.102, POCKET MAP C10/E3
Not far beyond the unfinished church of **San Marcuola** stands the Palazzo Vendramin-Calergi. Begun by Mauro Codussi at the end of the fifteenth century, this was the first Venetian palace built

Gondola on the Grand Canal near Palazzo Dario

Aerial view of the Basilica di Santa Maria della Salute

on classical Renaissance lines. The palazzo's most famous resident was Richard Wagner, who died here in February 1883. It's now the home of Venice's casino.

Ca' d'Oro

MAP P.102, POCKET MAP E10–11

Incorporating fragments of a thirteenth-century palace that once stood on the site, the gorgeous Ca' d'Oro was built in the 1420s and 30s, and acquired its nickname – "The Golden House" – from the gilding that used to accentuate its carving. (*Ca'* is an abbreviation of *casa di stazio*, meaning the main family home.) See page 79.

Ca' da Mosto

MAP P.102, POCKET MAP F11

The arches of the first floor of the Ca' da Mosto and the carved panels above them are remnants of a thirteenth-century Veneto-Byzantine building, and are thus among the oldest structures on the Canal Grande.

Fondaco dei Tedeschi

MAP P.102, POCKET MAP F12

Just before the Rialto Bridge stands the huge Fondaco dei Tedeschi. Now a schmaltzy shopping mall, it was once headquarters of the city's German merchants. In 1505 the Fondaco burned down; Giorgione and Titian were commissioned to paint the exterior. The remains of their contribution are now displayed in the Ca' d'Oro.

Palazzo Loredan and the Palazzo Farsetti

MAP P.102, POCKET MAP E13

The Palazzo Loredan and the adjoining Palazzo Farsetti are heavily restored Veneto-Byzantine palaces of the thirteenth century. They now both house the town hall.

Palazzo Grimani

MAP P.102, POCKET MAP E13

Work began on the immense Palazzo Grimani in 1559, to designs by Sanmicheli, but was not completed until 1575, sixteen years after his death. Ruskin, normally no fan of Renaissance architecture, made an exception for this colossal palace, calling it "simple, delicate, and sublime".

The Mocenigo palazzi

MAP P.102, POCKET MAP C14

Four houses that once all belonged to the Mocenigo family stand side by side on the **Volta del Canal**, as the Canal Grande's sharpest turn is known: the late sixteenth-century **Palazzo Mocenigo-Nero**; the double **Palazzo Mocenigo**, built in the eighteenth century as an extension; and the **Palazzo Mocenigo Vecchio**, a Gothic palace remodelled in the seventeenth century. Byron and his menagerie – a dog, a fox, a wolf and a monkey – lived in the Mocenigo-Nero for a couple of years.

Palazzo Grassi

MAP P.102, POCKET MAP C15

The vast palace round the Volta is the Palazzo Grassi, built in 1748–72 by Massari, who supervised the completion of the Ca' Rezzonico. The last great house to be built on the Canal Grande, it's now owned by the art collector and businessman François Pinault, and is used for exhibitions. See page 44.

Palazzo Franchetti and Palazzi Barbaro

MAP P.102, POCKET MAP C16–D16

The huge palazzo at the foot of the bridge is the Palazzo Franchetti, which was built in the fifteenth century and enlarged at the end

of the nineteenth. Its neighbours, on the opposite side of the Rio dell'Orso, are the twinned Palazzi Barbaro; the house on the left is early fifteenth century, the other late seventeenth-century. Henry James, Monet, Whistler, Browning and John Singer Sargent were among the luminaries who stayed in the older Barbaro house in the late nineteenth century.

Palazzo Corner della Ca' Grande

MAP P.102, POCKET MAP D16

The palace that used to stand on the site of the Palazzo Corner della Ca' Grande was destroyed when a fire lit to dry out a stock of sugar in the attic ran out of control. Sansovino's replacement, built from 1545 onwards, is notable for the rugged stonework of the lower storey – a prototype for Ca' Pésaro and Ca' Rezzonico.

Palazzo Contarini-Fasan

MAP P.102, POCKET MAP E16

The narrow Palazzo Contarini-Fasan – a mid-fifteenth-century palace with unique wheel tracery on the balconies – is popularly known as "the house of Desdemona", but although the model for Shakespeare's heroine did live in Venice, her association with this house is purely sentimental.

The double Palazzo Mocenigo

The northern islands

A trip out to the main islands lying to the north of Venice – San Michele, Murano, Burano and Torcello – will reveal the origins of the glass and lace work touted in so many of the city's shops, and give you a glimpse of the origins of Venice itself, embodied in Torcello's magnificent cathedral of Santa Maria dell'Assunta, which is one of the most charismatic buildings in the whole lagoon. These islands – especially Murano – attract a lot of visitors, but the voyage along the islet-dotted water-lanes of the northern lagoon – or even better, spending a night or two on beautiful Burano – can nonetheless be a great restorative, and the swathes of low-lying *barèna* (marshland) give a taste of what conditions must have been like for Venice's first settlers.

San Michele

MAP P.110, POCKET MAP J1–K2
Ⓦ comune.venezia.it/it/content/cimitero-smichele. Free.

The high brick wall around the island of San Michele gives way by the landing stage to the elegant white facade of **San Michele in Isola**, designed by Mauro Codussi in 1469. With this building Codussi quietly revolutionized the architecture of Venice, advancing the principles of Renaissance design in the city and introducing the use of Istrian stone as a material for facades. Easy to carve yet resistant to water, Istrian stone had long been used for damp courses, but

Gravestones at the cemetery island of San Michele

Boats to the islands

To get to the northern islands, the main vaporetto stop is **Fondamente Nove** (or Nuove), as most of the island services start here or call here. (You can hop on elsewhere in the city, of course – but make sure that the boat is going towards the islands, not away from them.) For **San Michele** and **Murano** only, the circular #4.1 and #4.2 vaporetti both run every twenty minutes from Fondamente Nove, circling Murano before heading back towards Venice; the #4.1 follows an anticlockwise route around the city, the #4.2 a clockwise route. Murano can also be reached by the #3 ("Diretto Murano"), which from around 8am to 6pm runs to the island from Tronchetto via Piazzale Roma and Ferrovia. For **Murano**, **Burano** and **Torcello** the #12 leaves every half-hour from Fondamente Nove for most of the day (hourly early in the morning and evenings), calling first at Murano-Faro before heading on to Mazzorbo and Burano, from where it proceeds, via Treporti, to Punta Sabbioni and the Lido. A shuttle boat runs every fifteen minutes between Burano and Torcello.

never before had anyone clad the entire front of a building in it; after the construction of San Michele, most major buildings in Venice were given an Istrian veneer.

The main part of the island, through the cloisters, is covered by the **cemetery** of Venice, established here by a Napoleonic decree which forbade further burials in the centre of the city. Space is at a premium, and most of the Catholic dead of Venice lie here in cramped conditions for just ten years or so, when their bones are dug up and removed to an ossuary, and the vacated plot is recycled. The city's Protestants, being less numerous, are permitted to stay in their sector indefinitely. In this Protestant section (no. XV) **Ezra Pound**'s grave is marked by a simple slab with his name on it. Adjoining is the Greek and Russian Orthodox area (no. XIV), including the gravestones of **Igor and Vera Stravinsky** and the more elaborate tomb for **Serge Diaghilev**.

Even with its grave-rotation system in operation, the island is reaching full capacity, and in 2017 an extension to a design by David Chipperfield was completed, comprising a sequence of formal courtyards clad in basalt and pietra d'Istria – the limestone from which much of Venice is built – and lined with wall tombs.

Murano

MAP P.110

Murano owes its fame entirely to its **glass-blowing industry**, and its main *fondamente* are crowded with shops selling the fruit of the furnaces, some of it fine, much of it repulsive. The rocketing fuel prices of the energy crisis had seen many of the glassmakers being forced to put a limit on how often and for how long their furnaces burn. Glass furnaces consume immense quantities of natural gas in order to function at consistent, high temperatures, that traditionally were maintained 24 hours a day. As we went to press, 80% of Murano's glassmakers had paused production.

From the Colonna vaporetto stop (the first after San Michele) you step onto the Fondamenta dei Vetrai, traditionally the core of the glass industry (as the name suggests) and now the principal tourist trap. Towards the far end is the Dominican church of **San Pietro Martire**, one of only two churches still in service on the island. Begun in 1363 but largely rebuilt after a fire in 1474, it contains a superb altarpiece by **Giovanni Bellini** and a couple of Paolo Veronese pictures.

Murano's museum is, as you'd expect, devoted to glass. Occupying the seventeenth-century Palazzo Giustinian (formerly home of the Bishop of Torcello), the **Museo del Vetro** (Ⓦ museovetro.visitmuve.it, charge) features pieces dating back to the first century and examples of Murano glass from the fifteenth century onwards. Perhaps the finest single item is the dark blue Barovier marriage cup, dating from around 1470; it's on show in room 2 on the first floor, along with some splendid Renaissance enamelled and painted glass. A separate display, with some captions in English, covers the history of

Murano glass techniques – look out for the extraordinary *Murrine*, the method of fusing and stretching differently coloured rods of glass.

The other Murano church is the wonderful **Santi Maria e Donato**. It was founded in the seventh century but rebuilt in the twelfth, and is one of the lagoon's best examples of Veneto-Byzantine architecture – the ornate rear apse being particularly fine. The glories of the **interior** are its mosaic floor (dated 1141 in the nave) and the twelfth-century mosaic of the Madonna in the apse. If you are staying on Murano, there are night visits on Wed at 9pm; email infovisitmurano@gmail.com for information.

Burano

MAP P.112

After the peeling plaster and eroded stonework of the other lagoon settlements, the small, brightly

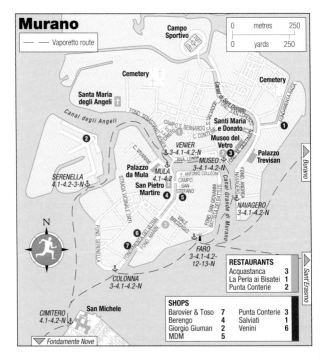

Murano

— Vaporetto route

Campo Sportivo

0	metres	250
0	yards	250

Cemetery

Cemetery

FONDAMENTA RADA

Santa Maria degli Angeli

Canal degli Angeli

Canal di San Donato

CAMPO S. BERNARDO

C. D. CRISTO

C. SAN SALVADOR

Santi Maria e Donato ❶

C. CONTERIE

Museo del Vetro ❸

2

VENIER ❷

RIVA. LONGA

C. VIVARINI

MUSEO 3-4.1-4.2-N

Palazzo Trevisan

Palazzo da Mula 4.1-4.2-N

MULA 4.1-4.2-N

F. ANTONIO COLLEONI

FOND. ANDREA NAVAGERO

San Pietro Martire ❹

CAMPO SAN STEFANO

❺

FOND. SERENELLA

SERENELLA 4.1-4.2-3-N ⚓

STRADA VICINALE DEI ORTI

FOND. SAN GIOVANNI BATTISTA DE BATTUTI

Canal Grande di Murano

NAVAGERO 3-4.1-4.2-N

Burano ▷

❻

❼

VIALE BRESSAGIO

FONDAMENTA DE VETRAI

FOND. MANIN

⚓

⚓

FARO 3-4.1-4.2-12-13-N

Sant'Erasmo ▷

N

COLONNA 3-4.1-4.2-N

CIMITERO 4.1-4.2-N ⚓

San Michele

▽ Fondamente Nove

RESTAURANTS

Acquastanca	3
La Perla ai Bisatei	1
Punta Conterie	2

SHOPS

Barovier & Toso	7	Punta Conterie	3
Berengo	4	Salviati	1
Giorgio Giuman	2	Venini	6
MDM	5		

Venetian glass

Allegedly because of the risk of fire – although many claim it was to protect the secrets of glassmaking from proto-industrial spies – Venice's glass furnaces were moved to **Murano** from central Venice in 1291, and thenceforth all possible steps were taken to keep the secrets of the trade locked up on the island. Although Muranese workers had by the seventeenth century gained some freedom of movement, for centuries prior to that any glass-maker who left Murano was proclaimed a traitor, and a few were even hunted down. A fifteenth-century visitor judged that "in the whole world there are no such craftsmen of glass as here", and the Muranese were masters of every aspect of their craft. They were producing spectacles by the start of the fourteenth century, monopolized the European manufacture of mirrors for a long time, and in the early seventeenth century became so proficient at making coloured crystal that a decree was issued forbidding the manufacture of false gems out of glass, as many were being passed off as authentic stones. The traditional style of Murano glass, typified by the multicoloured floral chandeliers sold in showrooms on Murano and round the Piazza, is still very much in demand. However, even before the 2020s fuel crisis, there was turmoil in the glass industry, due to an inundation of cheap Murano-style tableware and ornaments from Asia and eastern Europe. Very few of the surviving glassmakers are in Venetian hands – and most glassmakers have decided that the future will lie in prestige art and architectural projects. The best way of being sure to see a furnace at work is to book a tour in advance. Venezia Autentica (ⓦveneziaautentica.it), and My Venice Travel Guide (ⓦmyvenicetravelguide.it) both organise various kinds of glass-based experiences, some of which allow you to try your hand at simpler forms of glassmaking.

painted houses of Burano come as something of a surprise. Local tradition says that the colours once enabled each fisherman to identify his house from out at sea, but now the colours are used simply for pleasant effect. While many of the men of Burano still depend on the lagoon for their livelihoods, a lot of the island's women sell **lace**, though most of the lace in the shops is imported and machine-made. Real Burano lacemaking is still taught at the **Scuola del Merletto** (ⓦmuseomerletto.visitmuve. it, charge) on Piazza Baldassare Galuppi, which was opened in 1872, when the craft had declined so far that it was left to one woman, Francesca Memo, to transmit the

Artisanal processing of Murano glass

Santa Fosca church at Torcello

skills to a younger generation. Although the *scuola* is now almost moribund, a few courses are still held here, and pieces produced by its pupils and staff are displayed in the attached **museum**, along with specimens dating back to the sixteenth century.

Opposite the lace school stands the church of **San Martino**, with its drunken campanile; inside, on the second altar on the left, you'll find a fine *Crucifixion* by Giambattista Tiepolo.

Torcello

MAP P.112

Settled by the very first refugees from the mainland in the fifth century, Torcello became the seat of the Bishop of Altinum in 638 and in the following year its cathedral – the oldest building in the lagoon – was founded. By the fourteenth century its population had peaked at around twenty thousand, but Torcello's canals were now silting up and malaria was rife, and by the end of the fifteenth century Torcello was

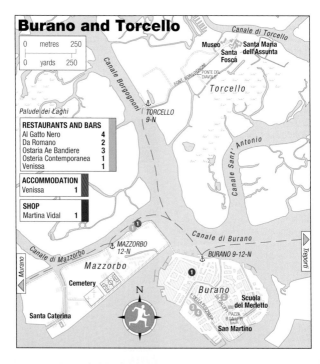

Burano and Torcello

0 metres 250
0 yards 250

Palude dei Laghi

RESTAURANTS AND BARS
Al Gatto Nero   4
Da Romano   2
Ostaria Ae Bandiere   3
Osteria Contemporanea   1
Venissa   1

ACCOMMODATION
Venissa   1

SHOP
Martina Vidal   1

Canale di Torcello

Museo   Santa Maria
Santa   dell'Assunta
Fosca

FONT. BORGOGNONI
PONTE DEL
DIAVOLO

Torcello

TORCELLO
9-N

Canale Borgognoni

Canale Sant' Antonio

Canale di Mazzorbo

MAZZORBO
12-N

Mazzorbo

Cemetery

Santa Caterina

Canale di Burano

BURANO 9-12-N

Treporti

Burano

Scuola
del Merletto

VIA S. MAURO
C. DELLA PESCHERIA
PIAZZA
B. GALUPPI

San Martino

Murano

The colourful houses of Burano

almost deserted. Today only eleven or so people remain in residence.

A Veneto-Byzantine building dating substantially from 1008, the **Cattedrale di Santa Maria dell'Assunta** (charge) has evolved from a church founded in the seventh century, of which the crypt and the foundations in front of the facade have survived. The dominant tones of the **interior** come from pink brick, gold-based mosaics and the watery green-grey marble of its columns and panelling, which together cast a cool light on the richly patterned eleventh-century mosaic floor. In the apse a stunning twelfth-century mosaic of the Madonna and Child looks down from above a frieze of the Apostles, which dates from the middle of the previous century. Below the window, at the Madonna's feet, is a much restored image of St Heliodorus, the first Bishop of Altinum, whose sarcophagus lies below the high altar. Mosaic work from the ninth and eleventh centuries adorns the chapel to the right of the high altar, while the other end of the cathedral is dominated by the tumultuous mosaic of the Apotheosis of Christ and the Last Judgement – created in the twelfth century, but renovated in the nineteenth. Ruskin described the view from the campanile as "one of the most notable scenes in this wide world", a verdict you can test for yourself (unless the tower is undergoing one of its frequent bouts of restoration).

Torcello's other church, **Santa Fosca** (free), was built in the eleventh and twelfth centuries for the body of the martyred St Fosca.

The nearby **Museo di Torcello** (servizimetropolitani.ve.it/en/torcello-museum/the-museum; charge) includes thirteenth-century gold figures, jewellery, mosaic fragments and a mishmash of pieces relating to the history of the area.

Shops: Murano glass

Barovier & Toso

MAP P.110
Fondamenta dei Vetrai 27–29 ⓦ barovier.com.
This family-run firm can trace its roots back to the fourteenth century. Predominantly traditional designs.

Berengo

MAP P.110
Fondamenta dei Vetrai 109a ⓦ berengo.com.
Berengo has pioneered a new approach to Venetian glass manufacture, with foreign artists' designs – ranging from Ai Wei Wei to Tracy Emin – being vitrified by Murano glass-blowers.

Giorgio Giuman

MAP P.110
Sacca Serenella, Murano ⓦ giuman.it.
Eccentric glassmaker with a foundry located off the beaten track, where you can usually drop in and visit without an appointment. Giuman makes any and everything from kitsch animals to lost-wax glass statues and is currently at work on a Greek-style glass temple which he plans to use as his mausoleum. This is a working foundry, and not really safe for children.

MDM

MAP P.110
Fondamenta Manin, 86
ⓦ mosaicidonamurano.com.
Mosaic tesserae and glass beads made in their factory on Murano ideal for anyone who wants to make their own mosaic or piece of jewellery.

Punta Conterie

MAP P.110
Fondamenta Marco Giustinian 1, Murano
ⓦ puntaconterie.com.
Occupying a former glass bead factory, Punta Conterie brings a fresh and contemporary note to Murano, favouring jewellery, clothes and objets by innovative – even iconoclastic – artists and designers.

Salviati

MAP P.110
Fondamenta Manin 56, Murano/
Fondamenta Lorenzo Radi 16, Murano
(Factory) ⓦ salviati.com.

Murano chandelier by Ercole Barovier and Toso, 1950s

Vase from the Venini workshop

Founded in 1859 by polymath, Antonio Salviati, who wanted to find a way to restore the mosaics of San Marco. Now one of the most prestigious glassmakers in Venice, Salviati collaborate with many leading designers and artists, and when working on a private commission no visitors are allowed. If you do get in, this is a place to see craftsmen work in the old way before visiting a stunning collection of glasswork ranging from limited edition perfume bottles for Dior and Armani, to stunning glass sculptures by Luciano Gaspari.

Venini

MAP P.110
Fondamenta Vetrai 47–48 Ⓦ venini.com.
One of the more adventurous producers, Venini often employs designers from other fields of the applied arts.

Shops: Burano lace

Martina Vidal

MAP P.112
Via San Mauro, 309 Burano
Ⓦ martinavidal.com.

One of the rare shops on Burano to commission lace from local craftswomen – indeed there is often a lacemaker at work – Martina Vidal and her brother Sergio have moved lacemaking on from doilies and petticoats to create contemporary linens, lighting and homeware. There is also tempting range of cashmere clothing. See the website for lacemaking courses.

Restaurants

Acquastanca

MAP P.110.
Fondamenta Manin 48, Murano
Ⓦ acquastanca.it.
A good-looking place (lots of bare wood, brick and marble) founded by two sisters-in-law, one who cooked for Harry's Bar, the other an architect with a passion for food. The menu is small but classy, with the emphasis on delicious and beautifully presented dishes using fresh fish and seafood. The front-of-house bar serves fine *cicheti*. €€€

Al Gatto Nero

MAP P.112
Fondamenta Giudecca 88, Burano
Ⓦ gattonero.com.

Tables at *Venissa*

This local trattoria has been run since the 1960s by Ruggero Bovo and his wife Lucia, helped by their son Massimiliano. What this family doesn't know about the lagoon's edible delicacies, and wines of the region, isn't worth knowing. €€€

Da Romano

MAP P.112

Via Galuppi 221, Burano Ⓦ daromano.it.
Huge and historic Burano restaurant, whose refined fish and seafood dishes have no lack of local devotees – the fish-broth risotto is famous and many local artists paid for their dinners with the painting on the walls. €€

La Perla ai Bisatei

MAP P.110

Campo San Bernardo 1e, Murano
☏ 041 739 528.
This is a basic but very good neighbourhood bar-trattoria, tucked into a corner of the island that very few tourists pass through.

Pasta dishes, risotto and a highly rated *frittura* form the core of the menu, and prices are amazingly low. €

Osteria Contemporanea

MAP P.112

Fondamenta Santa Caterina 3, Mazzorbo
Ⓦ venissa.it.
Venissa's more affordable and casual restaurant is a chic covered terrace that opens straight onto the vineyard. Their philosophy of 'environmental cuisine' – locally sourced sustainable produce – is realised in delicious dishes such as spaghetti using blue crab, an invasive species that threatens to obliterate local specialities such as vongole veraci (clams). €€€

Punta Conterie

MAP P.110

Fondamenta Marco Giustinian 1, Murano
Ⓦ puntaconterie.com.
Refined restaurant on a terrace at the angle of two canals which is the perfect place to escape the daily

day tripper infestation of Murano. Some truly astonishing dishes – try the fried okra in a panko crust with lime and basil served with cucumber marinated in kimchi and sriracha, or raw Sicilian tuna with slivers of young artichoke and nasturtium flowers. For a light lunch, gourmet sandwich or cake and coffee, they also run a Bistrot on the ground floor. €€€€

Venissa

MAP P.112
Fondamenta Santa Caterina 3, Mazzorbo
Ⓦ venissa.it.

On the island of Mazzorbo (connected to Burano by a foot bridge), the chefs of *Venissa* use the resources of the lagoon and the restaurant's own garden and vineyard to create a menu that mixes the traditional and the innovative to brilliant effect. The dining room is both stylishly zen and intimate (booking is essential), and there are tables outside in good weather. There are boutique rooms on the vineyard and the restaurant has its own boat, offering boat and restaurant packages from Marco Polo airport and from central Venice. If you are going to splash out on lunch anywhere in Venice, *Venissa* is arguably the most inspiring place to do so, proof that their commitment to 'environmental cuisine' – i.e to using whatever the lagoon and its islands offer – is no limit on taste or creativity. €€€€

Bar

Ostaria Ae Bandiere

MAP P.112
Via Giudecca, 114, Burano ⓘ 346 092 7700.
Pleasingly traditional canalside bar just off the beaten track, popular with locals of all ages, serving a couple of decent wines along with spritzes and cicheti. At its best in the early evenings.

Venetian *ciccheti* and wine

The southern islands

The section of the lagoon to the south of the city, enclosed by the long islands of the Lido and Pellestrina, has fewer outcrops of solid land than its northern counterpart. The nearer islands are the more interesting: the Palladian churches of San Giorgio and La Giudecca (linked by the #2 vaporetto) are among Venice's most significant Renaissance monuments, while the regeneration of the industrial buildings of La Giudecca, have given the island renewed vibrancy. The Venetian tourist industry began with the development of the Lido, which has now been eclipsed by the city itself as a holiday destination, yet still draws thousands of people to its beaches each year. A visit to the Armenian island, San Lazzaro degli Armeni, makes an absorbing afternoon's round-trip.

San Giorgio Maggiore

MAP P.120, POCKET MAP J8
ⓦ visitcini.com. Charge.

Palladio's church of San Giorgio Maggiore, facing the Palazzo Ducale across the Bacino di San Marco, is one of the most prominent and familiar of all Venetian landmarks. It is a startling building, both on the outside

and inside, where white stucco is used to dazzling effect – "Of all the colours, none is more proper for churches than white; since the purity of colour, as of the life, is particularly gratifying to God", wrote Palladio. Two outstanding pictures by **Tintoretto** hang in the chancel: *The Last Supper*, perhaps the most famous of all his works,

The church of San Giorgio Maggiore

Flooding and the barrier

Called the **acqua alta** (high water), the winter flooding of Venice is caused by a combination of seasonal tides, fluctuations in atmospheric pressure in the Adriatic and persistent southeasterly winds, and has always been a feature of Venetian life. In recent years, though, they have been getting worse and more frequent: in November 2019 the tide rose to 187cm above the mean, submerging about 80% of the city and causing wide-spread and long lasting damage. Even this was not quite as bad as the notorious flood of November 4, 1966, when for 48 hours the sea level remained an average of almost two metres above the mean high tide.

The idea of creating a tidal barrier was first mooted back in the 1980s, but it wasn't until 2003 that construction began. Known as **MOSE** (Moses) after the Old Testament's great divider of the waters, the barrier comprises 79 300-tonne steel flaps lying on the floor of the lagoon; when the water rises to dangerous levels, air is pumped into the flaps and the barrier floats upright. It was first put to the test in October 2020 and thankfully did what it was intended to do: while the sea-level on the outer side of the barrier reached 140cm above mean, in the city it remained at a manageable 60cm. All is not perfect, however. It takes hours to raise the barrier, and a sudden change in weather can lead to a severe flood, as happened in December 2020, just two months after MOSE was put into action for the first time. Critics argue that the project has actually exacerbated the situation, damaging the fragile lagoon and altering the flow of water with the construction of an artificial island off the Lido to house the technical buildings. On land, a host of less extravagant flood-prevention projects are underway, with embankments and pavements being raised at flood-prone points – in particular around San Marco – and the 60km of the lagoon's outer coastline being reinforced with stone groynes and artificial reefs to dissipate the energy of the waves. Many locals complain that MOSE is not used as often as it could be, and with global sea-levels set to rise, how long the anti-flood measures will be effective is uncertain.

and *The Fall of Manna*. They were painted as a pair in 1592–94 – the last two years of the artist's life, and a *Deposition* of the same date is in the Cappella dei Morti (charge). The door on the left of the choir leads to the **campanile** (charge), the best vantage point in Venice.

The adjoining monastery – now occupied by the **Fondazione Giorgio Cini**, which runs various arts institutes, a naval college and a craft school – is one of the city's architectural wonders, featuring two beautiful cloisters and a magnificent refectory by Palladio.

Exhibitions are regularly held here, and the Cini foundation run guided tours of the island, the Campanile, a beguiling labyrinth inspired by Borges, and a Greek style amphitheatre.

La Giudecca

MAP P.120, POCKET MAP B8–H9

La Giudecca is unlike anywhere else in Venice, a long chain of narrow islets linked by bridges that was, until the middle of the last century, the city's industrial powerhouse. Now a marvellous place to stay – as many a celebrity has discovered –

several of its factories and breweries have been renovated. Giudecca's nineteenth-century Gothic landmark, onetime flour mill, Molino Stucky, has become a *Hilton* hotel, a former granary has become a youth hostel, while other industrial buildings have been given new life as residential apartments and art studios. The Fortuny factory is here too, and continues to function, and although the factory is closed to visitors, you can usually pop into the showroom to take a look at the latest textiles. Anywhere else in the world, Giudecca's broad grid-like streets hung with washing strung between functional low-rise apartment blocks would be nothing special, but in Venice its very ordinariness can seem extraordinary; children playing in the street and locals chatting on corners, for example, are aspects of life that have long disappeared from the centre. With its radical working class traditions, there's a strong social conscience here too – if you are in Giudecca on a Thursday morning don't miss the little market on Piazza delle Convertite, selling fruit and vegetables grown by women in the island's prison (one of only four all-female prisons in Italy, housed in a former convent).

The first vaporetto stop after San Giorgio Maggiore is close to the tiny church of the **Zitelle**

(Ⓦ gioiellinascostidivenezia. it, charge), which was built in 1582–86 from plans worked out some years earlier by Palladio, albeit for a different site. Continuing along the waterfront you reach Palladio's Redentore and beyond it CREA, a series of artists' studios housed in a boatyard, the Cantiere Minore di Venezia, part of which is still functioning.

Il Redentore

MAP P.120, POCKET MAP F9
Ⓦ chorusvenezia.org. Charge.

La Giudecca's main monument is the Franciscan church of Il Redentore, designed by **Palladio** in 1577. In 1575–76 Venice suffered an outbreak of plague that killed nearly fifty thousand people – virtually a third of the city's population. The Redentore was built by the Senate in thanks for Venice's deliverance, and every year until the downfall of the Republic the doge and his senators attended a Mass here to renew their declaration of gratitude, walking to the church over a pontoon bridge from the Záttere. This is the most sophisticated of Palladio's churches, but an appreciation of its subtleties is difficult, as, unless you are lucky enough to find a kindly priest, a rope prevents visitors going beyond the nave. In the side chapels

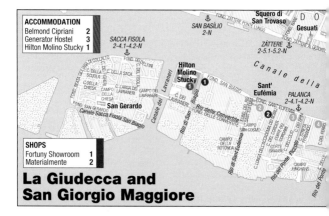

La Giudecca and San Giorgio Maggiore

View of Giudecca's Gothic landmark and former flour mill, Molino Stucky

you'll find a couple of pictures by Francesco Bassano and an *Ascension* by Tintoretto and his assistants, but the most astonishing feature is perhaps the fossil of a giant ammonite in the red marble.

The Lido

The Lido was an unspoilt strip of land until the latter part of the nineteenth century. Byron used to gallop his horses across its fields every day, and as late as 1869 Henry James could describe the island as "a very natural place". Before the century was out, however, it had become the smartest **bathing resort** in Italy, and although it's no longer as chic as it was, there's little room on its beaches in high season. The central stretch of sand used to be, in effect, the preserve of guests at the five-star hotels overlooking it, but a recent test case established that free access must be granted to all; you may, nonetheless, feel more welcome on the less groomed

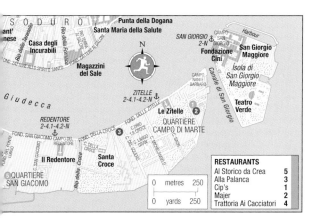

RESTAURANTS	
Al Storico da Crea	5
Alla Palanca	3
Cip's	1
Majer	2
Trattoria Ai Cacciatori	4

The Lido beach

public beaches at the northern and southern ends of the island.

In the vicinity of the Piazzale only the **Fortezza di Sant'Andrea** is of much interest, and you have to admire it from a distance across the water – you get a good view from the church and Franciscan monastery of **San Nicolò**. Founded in 1044, when there wasn't so much as a brick wall in this area, the church is notable for its splendid seventeenth-century choir stalls and a few scraps of mosaic that have survived from the eleventh-century building. A stroll along the nearby Via Cipro will bring you to the entrance to Venice's **Jewish cemetery** (for guided tours phone ☏ 041 715 359), which was founded in 1386 and in places has fallen into eloquent decay.

San Lazzaro degli Armeni

Ⓦ mechitar.org. Guided tours only, book via website. The #20 boat leaves San Zaccaria fifteen minutes before the tour starts and returns within ten minutes of the end.
No foreign community has a longer pedigree in Venice than the Armenians, whose presence is most conspicuously signalled by the island of San Lazzaro degli Armeni, identifiable from the city by the onion-shaped summit of its campanile. Tours are conducted by one of the priests who live in the island's **monastery**, and you can expect him to be trilingual, at the very least. Reflecting the encyclopedic interests of its occupants, the monastery is in places like a whimsically arranged museum: at one end of the old **library**, for example, a mummified Egyptian body is laid out near the sarcophagus in which it was found, while at the other is a teak and ivory throne that once seated the governor of Delhi. The monastery's collection of precious manuscripts and books – the former going back to the fifth century – is another highlight of the visit, occupying a modern rotunda in the heart of the complex. Elsewhere you'll see antique metalwork, extraordinarily intricate Chinese ivory carvings, a gallery of works by Armenian artists, a ceiling panel by the young Giambattista Tiepolo, and Canova's figure of Napoleon's infant son, which sits in the chamber in which Byron studied while lending a hand with the preparation of an Armenian–English dictionary. If you're looking for an unusual present, you could buy something at the shop: the old maps and prints of Venice are a bargain.

Shops

Fortuny showroom

MAP P.120, POCKET MAP C8
Fondamenta San Biagio 805
Giudecca. Appointments preferred.
🌐 venice@fortuny.com or ☏ 041 528 7697.

Mostly visited by wealthy home-owners and their interior designers, the Fortuny showroom is open to all and offers a fantastic opportunity for anyone interested in textiles to see the latest Fortuny creations – and perhaps indulge in a Fortuny umbrella (€850). Far more affordable is the range of notebooks covered with offcuts of Fortuny fabric.

Materialmente

MAP P.120, POCKET MAP D9
Calle del Forno 465c, Giudecca
🌐 materialmentevenezia.

Jewellery by goldsmith Maddalena Venier are perfectly realised miniature sculptures inspired the natural world and exquisite lighting designed by her partner Alessandro Salvadori. They work in Giudecca and sell from a tiny shop here and on the Merceria San Salvador 4850 San Marco.

Restaurants

Al Storico da Crea

MAP P.120, POCKET MAP E9
Imbarcadero del Redentore 212, Giudecca
☏ 041 296 0373.

Occupying light and airy upper-floor premises in the farthest reaches of Giudecca's biggest boatyard, this cheerful and good-value trattoria is all about fresh fish, seafood and game, and is popular with locals as well as tourists. For a fantastic view of the southern lagoon, reserve a table at the top of the steps. €€

Alla Palanca

MAP P.120, POCKET MAP E9
Fondamenta Ponte Piccolo 448, Giudecca
☏ 041 528 7719.

This no-frills trattoria, right by the Palanca vaporetto stop, is known

for traditional fish dishes such as sarde in saor and squid ink pasta. Eat inside at tables laid with paper mats, or – acqua alta permitting – outside on the fondamenta. Tramezzini too, if all you want is a quick bite and ombra at the bar. €€

Cip's

MAP P.120, POCKET MAP H9
Belmond Cipriani Hotel, Fondamenta San Giovanni, Giudecca.

The Cipriani's more casual bar-restaurant has a romantic, amber-lit terrace with views over the lagoon. Service is seamless, friendly and relaxed, and the cuisine simple enough to let the flavours of the primary ingredients shine through, yet sophisticated enough to make each mouthful unforgettable. Crispy quail comes with ginger and artichoke, a creamy baccalà mantecato in a crisp and unctuous crust. Lobster is served with clarified butter and all vegetables are grown on the island of Sant' Erasmo. €€€€

Majer

MAP P.120, POCKET MAP D7
Fondamenta Sant'Eufemia 461 Giudecca
🌐 majer.it.

Restaurant belonging to Venice's favourite artisan café chain offers some out of the ordinary dishes – many featuring Wagyu beef – as well as a beguiling selection of cicheti and miniature pastries if you just want a quick bite. Try the Cocoa Rigatoni with Jerusalem artichoke, broccoli, stracciatella, Bronte pistachio and fennel or a simple Chianina steak with grilled veg. Good wine list. €€€

Trattoria ai Cacciatori

MAP P.120, POCKET MAP E9
Fondamenta Ponte Piccolo 320, Giudecca
☏ 041 528 5849.

Cosy neighbourhood trattoria with cheery, welcoming staff who are still happy to see a tourist. Simple, inexpensive pasta and seafood dishes – try the spaghetti alle vongole, risotto or the fritto misto. Decent house wine. €€€

ACCOMMODATION

Interior of the luxury hotel *Danieli*

Accommodation

Venice has over a thousand hotels, but given the millions that visit every year, it can still be hard to find accommodation. We've indicated the minimum and maximum price for a standard double room; in high season – or during periods of high demand – prices will be at the highest end of the scale, though offers via hotel websites are common whenever occupancy is low. In addition, Venice has hundreds of bed and breakfast establishments (see page 133) and several thousand self-catering apartments (see page 133). Not all of them are official – which means the owners avoid paying local taxes – though the city council is determined to clamp down on these.

San Marco: North of the Piazza

AI DO MORI MAP P.36, POCKET MAP G14. Calle Larga San Marzo 658, Ⓦ hotelaidomori.com. Just a few paces off the Piazza, this has eleven simple rooms with white walls and wooden fittings on three floors with no lift (and no breakfast). The cheapest room has no ensuite bathroom, while the top-floor room has a private terrace looking over the Basilica, and understandably is the most expensive. €€

ANTICA LOCANDA AL GAMBERO MAP P.36, POCKET MAP F13. Calle dei Fabbri 4687, Ⓦ locandaalgambero.com. The *Antica Locanda* is in the heart of things, a short distance off the north side of the Piazza, and many of the 26 rooms – with brocade walls, gilt-framed mirrors and marble-tiled bathrooms – overlook a canal that's on the gondola route from the Bacino Orseolo. There's a popular restaurant on the ground floor. €€

CASA PETRARCA MAP P.36, POCKET MAP F14. Calle delle Schiavini 4386, Ⓦ casapetrarca.com. With rooms with and without ensuite facilities and air-con, this is one of the more reasonable hotels within a stone's throw of the Piazza – but make sure you book well in advance, as it only has seven rooms, including a tiny single. €€

PALAZZO ORSEOLO MAP P.36, POCKET MAP F14. Corte Zorzi 1083, Ⓦ palazzoorseolo.comlocandaorseolo. com. Abutting the Orseolo canal, north of the Piazza, this has rather plain, but spacious and light rooms, and the breakfasts substantial. The more expensive rooms have a view of the canal. Entrance is through an iron gate in Campo S. Gallo. €€

Accommodation price codes

Throughout this guide, accommodation prices have been quoted in the following categories, based on the price you would expect to pay per night including breakfast for a **double room in high season**.

€	under €100
€€	€100–200
€€€	€200–300
€€€€	€300–400
€€€€€	€400 and over

Tourist Tax

Tourist tax ranges from €1 to €5 euros per person per night, for the first five nights of any stay, and varies according to the time of year, the location and the type of accommodation. It is also levied on self-catering apartments. In an attempt to deter day-trippers – estimated at twenty million per year – there have been plans for some time to introduce a day-tripper tax. At the time of writing a pilot scheme is being mooted for 2024.

San Marco: West of the Piazza

ALA MAP P.42, POCKET MAP E15. Campo S. Maria del Giglio 2494, Ⓦ hotelala.it. A member of the Italian Una hotel group, the 85-room *Ala* has an adults only policy, and a nice location on a pretty Venetian campo that opens out onto a mouth of the Canal Grande. Rooms in both modern and traditional Venetian style. €€€

ART DECO MAP P.42, POCKET MAP D15. Calle delle Botteghe 2966, Ⓦ locanda artdeco.com. This cosy *locanda* has a seventeenth-century palazzo setting, but the interior features 1930s and 40s objects and the pristinely white bedrooms have modern wrought-iron furniture. No lift. €€

BLOOM MAP P.42, POCKET MAP D14. Campo Santo Stefano, 3470 San Marco, Ⓦ bloom-venezia.com. Beautiful rooms in a B&B run by hotel *Fiorita*, with parquet floors, white-limed beams and Fortuny lamps, spread over two floors of a pretty palazzo overlooking Campo Santo Stefano. Lush lounges and a wonderful roof terrace with a fridge close by to keep your wine cool. Complimentary bottle of prosecco on arrival but a very basic breakfast indeed. €€€

FIORITA MAP P.42, POCKET MAP D14. Campiello Nuovo 3457, Ⓦ locandafiorita. com. Charming place with just ten rooms furnished with brocades and antiques on a gorgeous little campiello off Campo Santo Stefano. The best rooms have little balconies overlooking the square. Rooms are all en suite and many are spacious. €€

FLORA MAP P.42, POCKET MAP E15. Calle dei Bergamaschi, off Calle Larga XXII Marzo 2283/a, Ⓦ hotelflora.it. Close to the Piazza, this family-run hotel has a delightful inner garden for breakfast or drinks. Rooms are beautifully decorated with period pieces, though some are a little small. €€

KETTE MAP P.42, POCKET MAP E15. Piscina S. Moisè, Ⓦ hotelkette.com. A favourite with the upper-bracket tour companies: the rooms are sizeable and luxuriously furnished, and it has a central yet quiet location, in an alleyway parallel to Calle Larga XXII Marzo, near La Fenice. Low season deals can be excellent! €€€

LA FENICE ET DES ARTISTES MAP P.42, POCKET MAP E15. Campiello Fenice 1936, Ⓦ fenicehotels.it. In business for more than a century, this seventy-room hotel has long been a favoured hangout of the opera crowd, performers and audience alike. Each room is individually decorated (some are all muted pastels, others are a riot of gold and scarlet) and there's also a small garden that's perfect for breakfast. €€€

MONACO AND GRAND CANAL MAP P.42, POCKET MAP F15. Calle Vallaresso 1332, Ⓦ monaco.hotelinvenice.com. The ground-floor rooms on the waterfront side of this famous and gorgeous hotel look over to the Salute and are kitted out in traditional Venetian style, with masses of Murano glass and great swags of brocade. In the annexe – the Palazzo Selvadego – you don't get a waterside view, but the decor is lighter, in a nouveau-Mediterranean style, with plain warm colours. €€€€

NOVECENTO MAP P.42, POCKET MAP D15. Calle del Dose 2683, Ⓦ novecento. biz. Intimate and very welcoming boutique *locanda* with nine individually decorated doubles, all with bathrooms. Styling is

Booking your accommodation

High season in Venice officially runs from March 15 to November 15 and then from December 21 to January 6, but most places don't recognize the existence of a low season any more. During these periods, and Carnevale, it's wise to book at least three months in advance, and for June, July and August it's virtually obligatory to reserve half a year ahead. Bear in mind, also, that many hotels – especially the smaller ones – require you to stay for a minimum of two or three nights in high season.

   Online agencies such as Ⓦvenicehotel.com and Ⓦbooking.com can have rooms available in hotels that are nominally full, and may even offer a discount on the hotel's quoted rate. The tourist office's website (Ⓦturismovenezia.it) gives details of accommodation of all types.

eclectic with furnishings from Morocco, Japan, China and Egypt, and there's a small courtyard for breakfast. €€€€

PALAZZINA GRASSI MAP P.42, POCKET MAP C14. Ramo Grassi 3247 San Marco, Ⓦpalazzinagrassi.com. Philippe Starck's deliberately disruptive makeover of the Grassi family's palazzina (or little palace) has seen the 24-room hotel become one of the addresses for parties during Carnevale and the Film Festival. Rooms are super-luxe and very sexy, while design – disconcerting objets and loads of mirrors – offer a conceptual workout after the easy-on-the-eye beauties of Venice. It has its own landing on the Grand Canal. €€€€€

Dorsoduro

ACCADEMIA VILLA MARAVEGE MAP P.50, POCKET MAP B16. Fondamenta Bollani 1058, Ⓦpensioneaccademia.it. Once the Russian embassy, this seventeenth-century villa has a devoted following, not least on account of its garden, which occupies a promontory at the convergence of two canals, with a view of a small section of the Canal Grande. The decor is traditional Venetian antique, with bare stone and wooden flooring. €€€

AMERICAN DINESEN MAP P.50, POCKET MAP C16. Fondamenta Bragadin 628, Ⓦhotelamerican.com. Nicely located, well-refurbished and welcoming hotel founded in the 1930s, with some rooms overlooking the Rio di San Vio, a couple of minutes' stroll

from the Accademia. There is a terrace on the first floor, a cocktail bar and it has its own dock for those arriving by boat. €€€€

CA' MARIA ADELE MAP P.50, POCKET MAP F7. Rio Terrà dei Catecumeni 111, Ⓦcamariaadele.it. Tatler called this lavishly over-the-top boutique hotel "wonderfully ridiculous, ridiculously wonderful" and each of its eleven rooms has its own distinctive take on exuberance, from the voluptuous boudoir feel of the 'Sala Noir' to the cool luxury of the 'Suite Barena'. The adjacent two-room B&B, Palazzetto 113, is similarly sybaritic, and similarly priced, while for those seeking total exclusivity, there is the three-storey Mini Palace, with its own landing stage and 10 metre-square roof terrace. €€€€€

CA' PISANI MAP P.50, POCKET MAP C16. Rio Terrà Foscarini 979a, Ⓦcapisanihotel.it. Rather glamorous 29-room hotel in a pretty fourteenth-century palazzo located just a few metres from the Accademia. Taking its cue from the 1930s and 40s, the Ca' Pisani makes heavy use of Art Deco walnut, curves and chrome, a refreshing break from the Renaissance and Rococo tones that tend to prevail in Venice's upmarket hotels. There is a roof terrace open for pre-dinner drinks, a Turkish bath (extra charge) and a restaurant. Some good last-minute deals via the website. €€

DD724 MAP P.50, POCKET MAP H16. Ramo da Mula 724, Ⓦthecharminghouse.com. Contemporary-styled boutique hotel right by the Guggenheim, with seven impeccably cool and luxurious rooms overlooking picturesque Rio Torreselle or the gardens of the Guggenheim. The same team runs nearby *DD694* with a spacious suite with lots of windows overlooking Rio Torreselle and pretty Campiello Barbaro, and three luxury suites in Palazzo Venier on Campiello Querini Stampalia, not far from San Marco. €€€€

LA CALCINA MAP P.50, POCKET MAP E8. Záttere ai Gesuati 780, ⓦ lacalcina. com. Reassuringly traditional hotel with a wide range of comfortable rooms located in pink canalside palazzo where Ruskin wrote much of *The Stones of Venice*. From the more expensive rooms you can gaze across to the Redentore, a church that gave him apoplexy. Each of the 29 rooms is uniquely furnished, but all have parquet floors – unusual in Venice. There are a handful of decent singles as well. Its restaurant (see page 60) is very good and has lovely canal views over to Il Redentore. €€€

PALAZZO EXPERIMENTAL MAP P.50, POCKET MAP A16. Fondamenta Zattere Al Ponte Lungo, 1411 Dorsoduro, ⓦ palazzoexperimental.com. The bold conversion of the former offices of the Adriatica Insurance Company into a super-cool hotel has resulted in one of Dorsoduro's most appealing new addresses. Not only as a place to sleep, but as a restaurant and cocktail bar as well. The cocktails have won prizes – as you might expect from a niche chain founded by two cocktail makers – but the restaurant is a winner too, with a small but well thought-out menu and excellent service. €€€€

PAUSANIA MAP P.50, POCKET MAP A15. Fondamenta Gherardini 2824 ⓦ hotelpausania.it. This quiet, comfortable hotel, occupies a fourteenth-century palazzo very close to San Barnaba church, just five minutes from the Accademia. There are 24 rooms of all shapes and sizes – including family rooms – some have frescoed ceilings, some overlook the San Barnaba canal, and others the pretty little internal garden. Lovely light public rooms and oodles of natural charm. Very good offers via the website. €€

San Polo and Santa Croce

CA' FAVRETTO-SAN CASSIANO MAP P.64, POCKET MAP D11. Calle della Rosa, Santa Croce 2232, ⓦ sancassiano. it. Classic Venetian style hotel with some rooms looking across the Canal Grande towards the Ca' d'Oro. Rooms have brocade walls and soft furnishing, gilded wood curlicues around mirrors and bedheads, and some have Murano glass chandeliers. There is also a nice courtyard garden, a grand entrance hall and the breakfast room has a balcony overhanging the canal. It was once the home of the nineteenth-century painter Giacomo Favretto. Prices vary enormously – the best deals (€) are to be had last-minute and six or more months in advance. €€€€

CA' SAN GIORGIO MAP P.64, POCKET MAP C10. Salizada del Fondaco dei Turchi 1725, Santa Croce, ⓦ casangiorgio. com. Exposed timber beams and walls of raw brick advertise the age of the Gothic palazzo that's occupied by this fine little *locanda*, while the bedrooms are tastefully and very comfortably furnished in gentle hues of cream and gold. The gorgeous top-floor suite has its own rooftop terrace. €€€

CA'SAN POLO MAP P.64, POCKET MAP C13. Calle de la Malvasia 2696, ⓦ casanpolo.it. Located in the heart of San Polo, this hotel is only steps away from the Church of Santa Maria Gloriosa dei Frari. Exposed beams and large windows and a very bright colour scheme make for cheery, cosy rooms, some with small balconies overlooking the rooftops of the city. €€

CIMA ROSA MAP P.64, POCKET MAP C10. Calle Tron 1958 Santa Croce, ⓦ cimarosavenezia.com. Upscale B&B created by a Venetian architect and his American wife, in a palazzo set right on the Grand Canal. You enter through a private walled courtyard garden into an atmospheric paved passage where ancient heavy oaken doors swing open onto a private gondola mooring. Rooms are painted in shades of lagoon greys, and most have canal views. A simple breakfast is served in the courtyard in good weather, and in the sitting room overlooking the canal in bad. €€€€

OLTRE IL GIARDINO MAP P.64, POCKET MAP B12. Fondamenta Contarini 2542, San Polo, ⓦ oltreilgiardino-venezia.com. This tranquil villa, formerly owned – briefly – by Alma Mahler, has been converted into an exquisite six-room hotel; the bedrooms – replete with antiques and works of art – are beautiful and airy, and there's a gorgeous little garden. €€

STURION MAP P.64, POCKET MAP E12. Calle del Sturion, San Polo 679, ⓦ locandasturion.com. The *Sturion* is one of an original 24 inns or *locande*, founded by the Venetian Republic in the thirteenth century – indeed the sign of the sturgeon appears in Carpaccio's *Miracle of the True Cross at the Rialto Bridge* (in the Accademia). The hotel is in a wonderful position overlooking the Canal Grande at the Rialto, but it is at the top of three flights of stairs and has no lift. Rooms are decorated with overpowering magenta brocade and some have Murano chandeliers. Good deals in low season, especially for rooms without a canal view. €€€

Cannaregio

ABBAZIA MAP P.76, POCKET MAP C3. Calle Priuli detta dei Cavalletti 68, ⓦ abbaziahotel.com. One of Cannaregio's most restful hotels, the *Abbazia* occupies a former Carmelite monastery (the monks attached to the Scalzi still live in a building adjoining the hotel) and provides comfortable rooms without losing its air of quasi-monastic austerity. There's a delightful internal garden where breakfast is service in good weather, the sitting room is in the former refectory – complete with lectern from which the bible would have been read during monkish mealtimes, and the staff are exceptionally helpful. €€€

AL PONTE ANTICO MAP P.76, POCKET MAP F12. Calle dell'Aseo, ⓦ alponteantico. com. This plush *residenza*, a few metres upstream of the Rialto Bridge, is decorated throughout in eighteenth-century style, with lashings of gold brocade, gilded wood and Murano glass. Classic and Superior rooms face inward, Deluxe rooms and Junior Suites have huge windows that open onto the Canal Grande, while the best room is the Junior Suite with patio overlooking the canal. €€€€

ANTICO DOGE MAP P.76, POCKET MAP F11. Sottoportego Falier, ⓦ anticodoge. com. Located within a stone's throw of the church of Santi Apostoli and overlooking the Santi Apostoli canal, this seven-room hotel occupies part of the palace that once belonged to the disgraced doge Marin Falier. Rooms have all the Venetian-style requisites: parquet floors, gilded bedheads, brocade walls with matching curtains. €€€€

GIORGIONE MAP P.76, POCKET MAP F10. Calle Larga dei Proverbi 4587, ⓦ hotelgiorgione.com. Very close to Santi Apostoli, this a more personal touch than many of the city's upmarket hotels – it has been run by the same family for many generations. Amenities include a quiet garden and a small saltwater pool – more suitable for cooling off with a cocktail than swimming – and some of the lavishly brocaded and gilded rooms have a small private terrace. €€€€

LOCANDA AI SANTI APOSTOLI MAP P.76, POCKET MAP F11. Strada Nova 4391a, ⓦ locandasantiapostoli.com. Occupying the top floor (no lift) of an ancient palazzo opposite the Rialto market, this little ten-room place has fresh white rooms with aggregate floors and ditsy florals, two of which overlook the Canal Grande – for which you'll pay a lot extra. The location terrific. €€€

LOCANDA DI ORSARIA MAP P.76, POCKET MAP C3. Calle Priuli dei Cavalletti 103, ⓦ locandaorsaria.com. Though it's situated close to the train station, this eight-room *locanda* is perfectly quiet. Some rooms are contemporary and others are decorated in a relatively understated version of Venetian Baroque. €€

LOCANDA LEON BIANCO MAP P.76, POCKET MAP F11. Corte Leon Bianco 5629, ⓦ leonbianco.it. Tucked away beside the crumbling old Ca' da Mosto, not far from the Rialto Bridge, with three of its eight rooms, overlooking the Canal Grande (for which there's a premium, of course). Some rooms pair flocked wallpaper with modern furniture, others are more contemporary. €€

MEZZO POZZO MAP P.76, POCKET MAP F11. Calle dei Preti 4529, ⓦ mezzopozzovenice.com. Pastel-hued rooms (with far less brocade than many) in a refurbished palazzo near Santi Apostoli. It's quite a haul up four flights of stairs, but most of the rooms are large. €€

PALAZZO ABADESSA MAP P.76, POCKET MAP F10. Calle Priuli 4011, ⓦ abadessa. com. *Residenza d'epoca* is a meticulously restored palazzo behind the church of Santa Sofia; all fifteen bedrooms (some of them huge) are furnished with genuine antiques, gilded frame mirrors, Murano chandeliers and damask wallpaper. There's a lovely secluded garden-patio. €€€€

Central Castello

AL LEON MAP P.88, POCKET MAP H14. Campo SS. Filippo e Giacomo 4270, ⓦ hotelalleon.com. Small, slightly dowdy hotel very close to the Piazza, with eleven heavily furnished rooms. €€

CANEVA MAP P.88, POCKET MAP G13. Corte Rubbi 5515, ⓦ hotelcaneva.com. A spartan, peaceful, inexpensive hotel tucked away behind the church of Santa Maria della Fava, close to Campo S. Bartolomeo. Most of the 23 rooms have a/c as well as private bathrooms. €€

CASA QUERINI MAP P.88, POCKET MAP H13. Campo S. Giovanni Novo 4388, ⓦ locandaquerini.com. Reasonably priced *locanda* in a quiet campo near the Piazza. Every room is different and you can have aperitivi and breakfast on a terrace in the campo in good weather. €€

CASA VERARDO MAP P.88, POCKET MAP H13. Calle della Chiesa 4766, ⓦ casaverardo.it. A fine hotel occupying a nicely refurbished sixteenth-century palazzo between San Marco and Campo Santa Maria Formosa. Antiquey public areas and twenty-three rooms – some brocade-and-flouncy others slicker and more contemporary – with a breakfast terrace downstairs, a small garden, a sun lounge at the top and another terrace attached to the priciest of the rooms. Customized mini bars – which means you can order whatever you like in advance! €€€

DANIELI MAP P.88, POCKET MAP H14. Riva degli Schiavoni 4196, ⓦ marriot.com. No longer the most exclusive or indeed expensive hotel in Venice, but many people feel that no other place can quite compete with the glamour of the *Danieli*, ever-iconic in its magnificent Gothic palazzo on the Canal Grande. Balzac stayed here, as did George Sand, Wagner and Dickens. €€€€€

PAGANELLI MAP P.88, POCKET MAP J6. Riva degli Schiavoni 4687, ⓦ hotelpaganelli.com. Refreshingly light, contemporary-styled rooms, especially if you get one of the rooms on the lagoon side – the ones in the annexe look towards S. Zaccaria, which is a nice enough view, but not quite in the same league. There are also less expensive, but still beautiful rooms on the ground floor and in a stylish annexe, and two more expensive rooftop rooms, each of which has a private terrace, one looking over Venice, the other overlooking the lagoon. There is a marvellous roof terrace for aperitivi with *cicchetti* by the hotel's partner restaurant, *Sestante*. €€€

PALAZZO CRISTO MAP P.88, POCKET MAP H11. Campo SSS Giovanni e Paolo 6805 ⓦ palazzocristo.com. Four sumptuous apartments, designed by interior designer Anna Covre and her architect husband on two floors of a palazzo overlooking Campo SS Giovanni e Paolo. Rooms are huge, light and magnificent, and the deft use of mirrors only adds to the sense of space and grace. Materials, fittings and furnishings are all meticulously sourced. The only drawback is you may never want to leave. €€€€€

Eastern Castello

INDIGO MAP P.98, POCKET MAP M8. Calle Buccari 10 Sant'Elena ⓦ indigovenice.com. The *Indigo* chain specializes in opening hotels in neighbourhoods most tourists ignore, and the *Indigo* Sant'Elena is no exception. Located in a former convent and school in a relaxed, leafy residential area beyond the Biennale gardens, it is the perfect choice for anyone wanting to escape the crowds, yet have San Marco in walking distance. Excellent aperitivi with *cicchetti* – and a very good restaurant indeed. €€€

Burano

VENISSA MAP P.112. Santa Caterina 3, Mazzorbo ⓦ venissa.it. *Venissa*'s answer to the Albergo Diffuso movement, a scattering of contemporary almost Scandinavian style conversions of typical island cottages run by the *Venissa* restaurant and vineyard. Either book by the room, or take an entire house. It's a wonderful way to experience the island – and within a day you'll be on nodding acquaintance with your neighbours. €€€

La Giudecca

BELMOND CIPRIANI MAP P.120, POCKET MAP H9. Giudecca 10, ⓦ belmond.com. Created in 1956 by *Harry's Bar* founder, Giuseppe Cipriani, as a haven for jetsetters, the *Cipriani* remains one of the finest addresses in Venice. Its location on the tip of Giudecca, far from the crowds, has only added to its appeal in recent years, and a complimentary shuttle boat means that dipping in and out the centre couldn't be easier. All 96 rooms have balconies, there's a seawater pool, clay tennis court, beautiful gardens and three restaurants. Breakfast is a feast with glorious variety (artisan bread, honey, fresh fruit, wafer thin slices of prized hams, the perfect eggs benedict) and service is faultlessly attentive. Rooms start at €1200 a night, but if you are going to push the boat out anywhere, this is the place. €€€€€

HILTON MOLINO STUCKY MAP P.120, POCKET MAP C8. Giudecca 810 ⓦ hilton. com. The *Hilton*'s conversion of Molino Stucky has given Venice its largest hotel yet. Rooms are comfy, interior spaces almost inevitably a little redolent of an airport lounge, but the advantages are the quiet location and (for a flat fee per person per stay of €15) regular boat shuttles with San Marco. Breakfasts are very good, though parents with young children may be appalled at the kids breakfast buffet – lollipops, M&Ms and a chocolate fountain. €€€€

Hostels

COMBO VENICE MAP P.76, POCKET MAP G3. Campo dei Gesuiti 4878, ⓦ thisiscombo.com. Contemporary hostel housed in a stunningly renovated convent, with a lively student vibe and programme of arts events. Lots of communal spaces, kitchens and ensuite rooms. Exposed brick walls, minimalist decor and a huge courtyard. Particularly great for anyone travelling alone. Buffet breakfast, bar with a canalside terrace, and a restaurant that serves inexpensive international food. €€

DOMUS CIVICA MAP P.64, POCKET MAP A12. Calle Campazzo, San Polo 3082 ☏ 041 721 103. This Catholic women's student hostel is open to tourists (including men) from mid-June to mid-September. Single, double, quad rooms with shared bathrooms; no breakfast; midnight curfew. Simple, clean, central and inexpensive. Discounts if you're staying for a week or more. €

FORESTERIA VALDESE MAP P.88, POCKET MAP H12. S. Maria Formosa, Castello 5170, ⓦ foresteriavenezia.it. Run by Waldensians, this hostel is installed in a wonderful palazzo at the end of Calle Lunga S. Maria Formosa, with flaking frescoes in the rooms and a large communal salon. It has bedrooms for one to four people and small; many of the smaller rooms have a private bathroom. Breakfast included. €

GENERATOR HOSTEL MAP P.120, POCKET MAP G9. Fondamenta delle Zitelle, Giudecca 86 ⓦ staygenerator.com. Occupies a superb location on Giudecca island looking over to San Marco. Rooms are bright, spacious and stylish, ranging from doubles to dorms (some female-only). Prices are higher than a standard hostel. Breakfast and sheets are included in the price – but remember to add the expense of the boat from central Venice. Dorms €, double rooms €€

OSTELLO SANTA FOSCA MAP P.76, POCKET MAP E2. S. Maria dei Servi, Cannaregio 2372, ⓦ ostellosantafosca.it. Student-run hostel in an atmospheric former Servite convent in a quiet area. Rudimentary rooms sleep two to seven people (some female-only), nearly all have shared bathrooms. 12.30pm curfew. €

B&Bs

The Italian tourism authorities define a bed and breakfast as an establishment with a maximum of three bedrooms available to paying guests, and a minimum of one shared bathroom for guests' exclusive use. The owners are supposed to live on site, the idea being that having a B&B should be a way of supplementing income and using spare rooms, but many people have used the B&B regulations to open small establishments and avoid the taxes exacted on mainstream hotels. Not that there is anything wrong with this at all, at least from a traveller's point of view, but take the precaution of booking through a website that will give protection if things are not as advertised. Prices tend to be lower than hotels – and some B&Bs are very special places indeed, where the owners have lovingly restored and created beautiful spaces in, perhaps, an apartment inherited from a parent or grandparent. Others are kitted out as cheaply as possible, but great if affordability is your priority. Many advertise on Airbnb, Ⓦ vrbo.com and Ⓦ booking.com. Three special B&Bs are:

CA' FUJIYAMA MAP P.50, POCKET MAP A15. Calle Lunga San Barnabà 2727a, Dorsoduro, Ⓦ fujiyamavenice.it. Carlo and Wenyu, the owners of this immaculate B&B, are perfect hosts, and have fitted out the plain rooms with a nod to Japanese and Chinese style. And this is perhaps the only B&B in Venice that serves real tea properly made – they have a little tearoom and breakfast is taken in the little garden. €€

DOMUS ORSONI MAP P.76, POCKET MAP C2. Calle dei Vedei 1045, Cannaregio, Ⓦ domusorsoni.it. This unusual B&B, close to the main Cannaregio canal, is attached to the Orsoni factory, which still manufactures glass mosaics. Each of the five smartly spartan rooms is adorned with a large Orsoni mosaic, and has a mosaic-tiled bathroom. €€€

RESIDENZA DE L'OSMARIN MAP P.88, POCKET MAP J5. Corte Rota 4960, Castello Ⓦ residenzadelosmarin.com. Charming Venetian house on a narrow canal between San Marco and San Giorgio dei Greci, with three restful, stylish rooms. The third-floor room is the most enviable – with a private roof terrace looking down on the canal – and one of the second-floor rooms has a small terrace overlooking the courtyard. Breakfast is served on the terrace in good weather and features home-made cakes. No lift. €€€

Apartments

The very high cost of hotel rooms in Venice makes self-catering an attractive option to many. Airbnb has over a thousand listings, to the despair of local residents and the mayor, who see their city overrun with tourists, while it becomes increasingly impossible to find rentals for themselves. Rentals to tourists are strictly limited to 90 days or less.

Venetian Apartments Ⓦ veniceprestige.com. An offshoot of Sothebys, this site has more than a hundred upscale apartments in the city, ranging from very cool studios to an extraordinarily sumptuous palazzo on the Canal Grande.

Venice Apartment Ⓦ veniceapartment.com. An Italian website with more than 150 properties on its books.

Views on Venice Ⓦ viewsonvenice.com. Well-established company with over eighty luxurious and privately-owned apartments, and very good service on the ground.

VRBO Ⓦ vrbo.com. This site – which puts you in touch directly with the owners – features hundreds of properties in Venice and the Veneto.

ESSENTIALS

Painting of the Bacino di San Marco, Antonio Joli (c. 1742)

Arrival

Marco Polo airport

Most scheduled flights and some charters arrive at Marco Polo (ⓦveniceairport.it), around 7km north of Venice, on the edge of the lagoon. The most inexpensive way into town is to take one of the two road-going **bus services** to the terminal at Piazzale Roma: the ATVO (Azienda Trasporti Veneto Orientale; ⓦatvo.it; tickets available online) coach, which departs every half-hour and takes around twenty minutes, or the ACTV (Azienda del Consorzio Trasporti Veneziano; ⓦactv.avmspa.it) bus #5, which is equally frequent, costs the same and usually takes just five minutes longer (it's a local bus service, so it picks up and puts down passengers between the airport and Piazzale Roma). The main advantage of this bus is that you can opt for an Aerobus più Nave ticket which includes transfer to a vaporetto once you arrive in Venice. You save a little bit of money, but more importantly, avoid the ticket queues.

A far more appealing option is to approach the city by water on one of the Alilaguna **water-buses** (ⓦalilaguna.it), which operate on three routes from the airport: the Blu line, via Murano, Fondamente Nove, Lido, San Zaccaria, San Marco, Záttere, Giudecca and Terminal Crociere (the docks); the Arancia (Orange), via Madonna dell'Orto, Guglie, San Stae, Rialto, Sant'Angelo, Ca' Rezzonico and San Marco; and the Rosso (Red), via Murano to the Lido (April–Oct). The fare is €15 to any stop in central Venice, and €8 to Murano. All services are hourly, and the journey time to San Marco is about 1hr 10min. **Ticket offices** for Alilaguna are on the dock, and

for ACTV and ATVO services in the arrivals hall; in addition to single tickets, you can also get returns or ACTV passes here – a wise investment for almost all visitors. Note that ACTV passes are not valid on the Alilaguna service nor on the ATVO bus.

The most luxurious mode of transport is a **water-taxi**. The drivers tout for business in and around the arrivals hall, and will charge in the region of €140 to central Venice for up to six people, with supplements charged if your journey involves one of the more difficult-to-navigate canals. Book and check prices in advance at ⓦmotoscafivenezia.com. Ordinary **car-taxis** cost about €60 to Piazzale Roma.

Treviso airport

Treviso airport is used chiefly by **charter** companies, some of which provide a free bus link from the airport into Venice. An ATVO bus service to Venice's Piazzale Roma meets the incoming Ryanair flights; the fare is only a couple of euros more than the Marco Polo-Venice bus fare, and the journey takes 1hr 10 min. Much quicker are the Barzi buses that run 10–15 times daily from Treviso airport to Piazzale Roma – they cost the same and they take just 40 minutes.

By road and rail

Arriving by **train**, **coach or bus**, you simply get off at the end of the line. The **Piazzale Roma** bus station and **Santa Lucia** train station (not to be confused with Venezia Mestre, the last stop on the mainland) are just a couple of minutes' walk from each other at the top of the Canal Grande.

Getting around

With the exceptions of the #1, #2 and the night service, the water-buses skirt the city centre, connecting points on the periphery and the outer islands. Taking a water-bus is usually the quickest way of getting between far-flung points, but in many cases the speediest way of getting from A to B is on foot – you don't have to run, for instance, to cover the distance from the Piazza to the Rialto Bridge more quickly than the #1 boat. Once you've got your bearings navigation is not as daunting as it seems at first. Yellow signs posted high up on streetcorners all over central Venice indicate the main routes to San Marco, Ferrovia (train station) and Rialto. For public transport enquiries ACTV have an office at Piazzale Roma or ⌾actv.it.

Water-buses

There are two types of water-bus: the **vaporetti**, which are the workhorses used on the Canal Grande services (#1 and #2) and other heavily used routes; and the smaller **motoscafi**, which are employed on routes where the volume of traffic isn't as great (notably the two "circular routes" – #4.1/4.2 and #5.1/5.2).

The standard **fare** is exorbitant (€9.50 for a single journey); the ticket is valid for 75 minutes, and for any number of changes of water-bus, but cannot be used as a return ticket. There are reduced tickets for one-stop hops across the Canal Grande, or between San Zaccaria and San Giorgio Maggiore, or the Lido and Sant'Elena. If you have more than one piece of large luggage, there is a charge for each additional item. Children under 4 travel free on all public transport. If you are not using Chat&Go on your phone, **tickets** are available from most landing stages, shops displaying the ACTV sign, and all the tourist offices; the travel passes are available from the tourist offices and at the Piazzale Roma, train station, Ca' d'Oro, Rialto, Accademia, San Marco Vallaresso, San Zaccaria, Arsenale, Záttere, Fondamente Nove and Tronchetto vaporetto stops. In the remoter parts of the city you may not be able to find anywhere to buy a ticket, particularly after working hours, when the booths at the landing stages tend to close down; tickets can be bought on board at the standard price, as long as you ask the attendant as soon as you get on board; if you delay, you could be liable for a hefty spot-fine.

Unless you intend to walk all day, you may save money with a Venezia Unica **travel card** (see above). ACTV

Chat & Go Smart Transport Ticketing

Although you can buy tickets directly on the vaporetto, there is a an efficient smartphone ticketing system that operates either via the WhatsApp number (☎39 339 990 8002) or by scanning the QR codes displayed at all vaporetto and bus stops. To pay you either need to have registered a credit or debit card in your phone, or use Android Pay or Apple Pay. Tickets available are the urban ticket valid for 75 minutes for buses, tram and the People Mover; the Aerobus ticket; and the standard rete unica ticket (valid for 75 minutes on the entire urban network including vaporetti, bus, tram and the People Mover, but excluding travel to and from Marco Polo Airport).

Venezia Unica & Rolling Venice

For tourists who intend to do some intensive sightseeing, the city has a ludicrously complicated scheme called **Venezia Unica** (Ⓦveneziaunica.it), in which you choose a menu of services online (museum passes, water-buses, wi-fi networks, public toilets etc), and are then quoted a price for a ticket that also includes discounts to some other museums and exhibitions. The best deals are for cards purchased at least 30 days in advance. The process is explained in English on the website, but be prepared for it to take some time for you to work out what suits your needs best. You could, for example, decide to limit your Venezia Unica card to waterbuses only, ranging from a single journey to 7 days.

If you're aged between 6 and 29, you are eligible for a **Rolling Venice** card, which gives you some discounts at certain shops, restaurants, museums and exhibitions (details are given in a leaflet that comes with the card) and entitles you to a heavily discounted 72-hour ACTV travel pass (not valid for the airport bus).

The **Venezia Autentica Friends' Pass** (Ⓦveneziaautentica.com) gives visitors discounts at artisan shops all over the city.

---

produces tickets valid for **24 hours**, **48 hours**, **72 hours**, and (best value of all) **seven days**, which can be used on all ACTV services within Venice. A supplement is payable if you want to use an ACTV pass on the airport buses.

All pre-purchased tickets and travel passes must be **validated** before embarking, by swiping the card or phone across one of the machines at the entrance to the vaporetto stop. Forgetting to swipe can incur a fine.

Water-bus routes

What follows is a run-through of the water-bus routes that visitors are most likely to find useful; a full **timetable** can be downloaded from Ⓦactv.it and can usually be picked up at the Piazzale Roma, Ferrovia, San Marco, San Zaccaria, Accademia and Fondamente Nove vaporetto stops.

Be warned that so many services call at **San Marco**, **San Zaccaria**, **Rialto** and the **train station** that the stops at these points are spread out over a long stretch of waterfront, so you might have to walk past several stops before finding the one you need. Note that the main San Marco stop is also known as **San Marco Vallaresso**, or plain Vallaresso, and that the San Zaccaria stop is as close to the Basilica as is the Vallaresso stop. There is a user-friendly interactive map at Ⓦactv. avmspa.it/sites/default/files/avm/ navigazione/MAP/interattiva.html.

#1

The slowest of the water-buses, and the one you'll use most often. It starts at Piazzale Roma, calls at every stop on the **Canal Grande** except San Samuele, works its way along the **San Marco** waterfront to **Sant'Elena**, then goes over to the **Lido**. The #1 runs every 20min 5–6.20am, every 10min 6.20am–10pm and every 20min 10–11.40pm. For the night service, see #N.

#2

The timetable of the #2 is immensely complicated, but basically from around 9am to 5pm its clockwise route takes it from San Zaccaria to San Giorgio Maggiore, Giudecca (Zitelle, Redentore and Palanca), Záttere, San Basilio,

Sacca Fisola, Tronchetto, Piazzale Roma, the train station, then down the Canal Grande (calling only at Rialto, San Tomà, San Samuele and Accademia) to San Marco Giardinetti; the anti-clockwise version calls at the same stops. It runs in both directions every 12min. From around 5–9am and 5–11.30pm, however, the lower section of Canal Grande is omitted, so the #2 runs back and forth between San Zaccaria and Rialto, every 20min. In summer the #2 is extended out to the Lido, via Giardini.

#4.1/4.2

The **circular service**, running right round the core of Venice, with a short detour at the northern end to **San Michele** and **Murano**. The #4.1 travels anticlockwise, the #4.2 clockwise and both run every 20min from about 6.10am–7.30pm; before and after that, the #4.1/4.2 together act as a shuttle service between Murano and Fondamente Nove, running every 20min from 4.30am until around 11.20pm.

#5.1/5.2

Similar to the #4.1/4.2, this route also **circles Venice**, but heads out to the **Lido** (rather than Murano) at the easternmost end of the circle. The #5.1 runs anticlockwise, the #5.2 clockwise, and both run fast through the Giudecca canal, stopping only at Záttere and Santa Marta between San Zaccaria and Piazzale Roma. Be aware that in the early morning and late evening neither service does a complete loop of the city.

#12

For most of the day, from 4.30am, the **#12** runs every half hour from Fondamente Nove (approximately hourly after 8.40pm), calling first at **Murano-Faro** before heading on to **Mazzorbo**, **Burano** (from where there

is a connecting half-hourly shuttle to Torcello), and Treporti; it runs with the same frequency in the opposite direction.

#3

From around 6am to 6pm the **#3** runs from Piazzale Roma to Murano, where it always calls at Colonna and Museo, and often at other Murano stops too.

#N

This **night service** (11.30pm–4.30am) is a selective fusion of the #1 and #2 routes. Other night services connect Fondamenta Nuova with Murano, and with Burano, Torcello and Punta Sabbioni.

Traghetti

Traghetti (gondola ferries also known as gondola-parada) are the only cheap way of getting a ride on a gondola, albeit a stripped-down version, with none of the trimmings and no padded seats – most Venetians stand up. There used to be almost thirty gondola traghetti across the Canal Grande but today there only San Tomà-Sant'Angelo functions with any kind of regularity. That said, it is always worth a look if you are passing one of the stations (Dogana, Riva del Carbon, Riva del Vin, S, Sofia)

Gondolas

The gondola, once Venice's chief form of transport, is now purely an adjunct of the tourist industry. But however much the gondola's image has become tarnished, it is an astonishingly graceful craft, perfectly designed for negotiating the tortuous and shallow waterways, and an hour's slow voyage through the back canals can give you a wholly new perspective on the city.

To hire a gondola costs €90 per thirty minutes for up to six passengers, rising to €110 (35 minutes) between 7pm and 8am; you pay an extra €50 for every additional twenty minutes, or €60 from 7pm to 8am. Further hefty surcharges will be levied should you require the services of an on-board accordionist or tenor. Even though the tariff is set by the local authorities, it's been known for gondoliers to extort even higher rates than these – if you do decide to go for a ride, establish the charge before setting off. To minimize the chances of being ripped off by a private individual making a few dozen euros on the side (and there are plenty of those in Venice), take a boat only from one of the following official gondola stands: west of the Piazza at Calle Vallaresso, Campo San Moisè or Campo Santa Maria del Giglio; immediately north of the Piazza at Bacino Orseolo; on the Molo, in front of the Palazzo Ducale; outside the *Danieli* hotel on Riva degli Schiavoni; at the train station; at Piazzale Roma; at Campo Santa Sofia, near Ca' d'Oro; at San Tomà, to the east of the Frari; or by the Rialto Bridge on Riva Carbon.

Taxis

Venice's **water-taxis** are sleek and speedy vehicles that can penetrate all but the shallowest of the city's canals. Unfortunately they are possibly the most expensive form of taxi in Europe: the clock starts at €15 and goes up €2 every minute. All sorts of additional surcharges are levied as well: €10 for each extra person if there are more than five people in the party; €5 for each piece of luggage in excess of five items; €20 for a ride between 10pm & 7am. There are five ways of getting a taxi: go to one of the main stands (at Piazzale Roma, the train station, Rialto and San Marco Vallaresso), find one in the process of disgorging its passengers, call one by phone (☎ 041 522 2303), email at ✉ info@ motoscafivenezia.it or book through ⌨ motoscafivenzia.it.

Directory A–Z

Accessible travel

It might be easy to assume that a city with more than 400 bridges (most of them stepped) would offer unsurmountable obstacles to wheelchair users. Thankfully this is not the case. Key bridges are fitted with wheelchair lifts and an increasing number of smaller bridges are fitted with ramps. Wveneziaunica.it has a link to a series of 14 wheelchair-friendly itineraries in the city, designed by the Office for the Elimination of Architectural Barriers along with people with mobility needs who live in the city and want to make their daily life experience available to everyone. At the time of writing the itineraries are only available in Italian, but pasting them into Google translate produces a reasonably comprehensible translation, as long as you bear in mind that 'campo' literally means field! Getting on and off the water-buses can be difficult – even hazardous – especially at low tide or when the canals are choppy, but boat staff are on hand to help. At rush hour, wheelchair users may prefer to avoid the smaller boats where there is just a small area for passengers at deck level, with the main seating area is below deck (#4.1, #4.2, €5.1, #5.2). Note that captains of these smaller boats are not obliged to accept passengers with wheelchairs. The boats used by lines #1 and #2 are much more accessible, but can be a nightmare at peak times. Many smaller hotels and B&Bs occupy upper storeys without lifts, so be sure to check accessibility before booking.

Children

Families with young children may find life easier staying in one of the more residential neighbourhoods away from the crowds of tourists; Sant'Elena in Eastern Castello is an excellent choice (and has one of the city's few playgrounds). Giudecca also has plenty of broad streets and squares, with local kids playing outside. Closer to the centre, Santa Croce, particularly around Campo San Giacomo dell'Orio has a buzzy neighbourhood feel, and again, is somewhere you'll often see local children playing outside. If bringing a pram or pushchair, it's worth taking a look at the 14 wheelchair-friendly itineraries mentioned in our section on accessible travel. The Guggenheim – with audioguides for children – and the Querini-Stampalia – with a child-friendly itinerary and information boards – are two of the most enjoyable museums to visit with kids, while the prisons of the Palazzo Ducale, the ships of the Museo Storico Navale, and the recently revamped Museo di Storia Naturale are also likely to appeal. And if you need to escape the city and have down-time on a beach, the sands of the Lido are just a boat-hop away.

Crime and Emergencies

For police emergencies ring T113. Alternatively, dialling ☎ 112 puts you straight through to the Carabinieri (military police), ☎ 115 goes straight to the Vigili del Fuoco (fire brigade) and ☎ 118 straight to Pronto Soccorso Medico (ambulance). As you might imagine, petty theft and pickpocketing is rife, and the combination of jostling crowds and the ease of making a swift disappearance into a labyrinth of alleyways makes for easy pickings. Be vigilant. Cover the ATM keyboard with your hand if you have to tap out your PIN; don't carry cash and cards together; and if using your phone to pay, make sure you put it back somewhere you can keep a hand on it. Be wary of people who look very obviously touristy – carrying a rucksack on your front and holding a paper map can be a scam to hide what hands are doing. Likewise, floppy hats and scarves can be used to hide faces from security cameras. Look as if you know where you are going, even if you don't. To notify police of a theft or lost passport, report to the Questura, which is at Rampa Santa Chiara 500, on the north side of the road bridge that leads onto Piazzale Roma (☎ 041 271 5511, ☺ questure.poliziadistato.it). There's a small local police (polizia urbana) station on the Piazza, at no. 63.

Discount passes

The Musei di Piazza San Marco card gives access to the Palazzo Ducale, Museo Correr, Museo Archeologico and Palazzo Ducale. The Museum Pass gives access to all those plus the all the other civic museums (☺ visitmuve.it for both cards). The Chorus Pass (☺ chorusvenezia.org) gives access to eighteen churches including the Redentore, Santa Maria Formosa and Santa Maria dei Miracoli. For those planning an intense bout of sightseeing, the Byzantine complexities of the Venezia Unica scheme may be worth consideration (☺ veneziaunica.it). From the online menu you select a combination of museum passes, public transport, airport transfers and car-parking fees. Note that the best deals are for those who book over 30 days in advance. Anyone between the ages of 6 and 29 is eligible for a Rolling Venice card, which includes a sizeable discount on a 72-hour ACTV travel pass, along with further discounts at participating shops, restaurants, museums and exhibitions (☺ veneziaunica.it).

Embassies & consulates

Australia: Australian Consulate General Ⓦ italy.embassy.gov.au
Canada: Canadian Consulate Ⓦ canadian-consulate.com
New Zealand: Consulate General Ⓦ mfat.govt.nz
Republic of Ireland: Honorary Consulate, Ⓦ dfa.ie
UK: British Consulate General Ⓦ british-consulate.org
US: US Consulate General, Ⓦ it.usembassy.gov

Electricity

The supply in Italy is 220V, though anything requiring 240V will work. Most plugs have two round pins, but the sizes can vary (even some Italian plugs need adapters): UK equipment will need an adaptor, US equipment a 220-to-110 transformer as well.

Health

All EU countries have reciprocal arrangements for reclaiming the costs of medical services. UK residents can get a Global Health Insurance Card free from the NHS (Ⓦ nhs.uk) but be aware that this will only entitle you to state-provided emergency medical care, visits to A&E, maternity care (unless you are going abroad to give birth) and you may have to pay costs up front and claim them back, so be sure to get receipts for all treatment and medicines. UK and all non-EU members are advised to have private travel insurance that covers medical care, emergency repatriation costs and additional expenses such as accommodation and flights for anyone travelling with you.

Hospital

Ospedale Civile, Campo SS. Giovanni e Paolo ☏ 041 529 4111.

Internet access

Most hotels offer free wi-fi. Free wi-fi in cafes is less common.

Left luggage

There's a left luggage office at Piazzale Roma and another beside platform 1 at the train station.

LGBTQ+ travellers

There is not much of any kind of gay scene in Venice, though attitudes are liberal and there is no need to dress or behave any differently to how you would at home.

Lost property

If you lose anything on the train or at the station, call ☏ 041 785 531; at the airport call ☏ 041 260 9226; on the water- or land buses call ☏ 041 272 2179; and anywhere in the city itself call ☏ 041 274 8225.

Money

You can save money by walking rather than taking waterboats, and if you come across a little local bar or restaurant where you can drink and eat inexpensively, treat it like gold, and go back as often as you can. Banks are concentrated around Campo San Luca and Campo Manin (in the north of the San Marco *sestiere*). Hours are generally Mon–Fri 8.30am–1.30pm and then for an hour in the afternoon. There are clusters of exchange bureaux (*cambio*) near San Marco, the Rialto and the train station. Open late every day of the week, they can be useful in emergencies, but their rates of commission and exchange tend to be steep.

Museums and monuments

There are two **Museum Cards** for the city's civic museums (Ⓦ visitmuve.it). The **Musei di Piazza San Marco** card costs €30/15 (discount for students under 30, EU citizens over 65 & Rolling Venice Card holders), and gets you into the Palazzo Ducale, Museo Correr, Museo Archeologico and the Biblioteca Marciana; it's valid for three months.

The **Museum Pass**, costing €41/23, covers these four, plus all ten other civic museums: Ca' Rezzonico, Casa Goldoni, Palazzo Mocenigo, Museo di Storia Naturale, Ca' Pésaro (the modern art and oriental museums), the Museo del Merletto (Burano) and the Museo del Vetro (Murano). It's valid for six months. Both passes allow one visit to each attraction and are available online or from any of the participating museums. The Palazzo Ducale and Museo Correr can be visited only with a museum card; at the other places you have the option of paying an entry charge just for that attraction. Accompanied disabled people have free access to all civic museums.

Eighteen churches are part of the ever-expanding **Chorus Pass** scheme (⊚ chorusvenezia.org), whereby a **€14 ticket** allows one visit to each of the churches over a one-year period. The proceeds from the scheme are ploughed back into the maintenance of the member churches; the individual entrance fee at each church is €3.50. Opening hours are listed throughout the guide, but bear in mind that the times are prone to sudden alteration, especially in winter, and that many of the less-visited churches are often shut because people can't be found to keep them open. The churches involved are: the Frari; the Gesuati; the Redentore; San Giacomo dell'Orio; San Giobbe; San Giovanni Elemosinario; San Pietro di Castello; San Polo; San Sebastiano; San Stae; Sant'Alvise;

Santa Maria dei Miracoli; Santa Maria del Giglio; Santa Maria Formosa; Santo Stefano; San Vidal; San Giacomo di Rialto; San Giuseppe di Castello. The Chorus Pass is available at each of these churches, and the tourist offices.

Opening hours

Traditional opening hours for shops in Italy are 8 or 9am until 1pm, and then from 3 or 4pm until 7 or 8pm, but these days in Venice most shops (except food shops) open at around 10am until 8pm. Supermarkets tend to open earlier (8 or 8.30am and stay open until 7 or 8pm). Only the occasional family-run neighbourhood grocery or wine shop will close for lunch. It is impossible to generalise about museum opening times, but the most museums closed one day per week, usually Monday or Tuesday. Church opening times are also impossible to generalise, but many close for several hours from noon or 1pm, re-opening at around 3pm in winter and 4pm or later in summer.

Post offices

Venice's central **post office** is at Marzaria San Salvador 5015. Branch offices are located throughout the city including at Calle dell'Ascensione 1241 (off the west side of the Piazza), Calle del Spezier 233 and Campo San Polo 2022 (in Dorsoduro), and Via Garibaldi 1641 (Castello). Other branches listed at ⊚ poste.it/cerca/index.html#/ vieni-in-poste/Venezia are all open

---

Eating out price codes

Throughout this guide, restaurant prices have been quoted in the following categories, based on the usual cost of a two-course meal for one person, including a drink.

€€€€	€80 and above
€€€	€50–80
€€	€25–50
€	under €25

Useful websites

Ⓦ **churchesofvenice.com** Jeff Cotton's wonderful website is replete with fascinating facts and stories about the churches of Venice, Verona and Padua.

Ⓦ **iamnotmakingthisup.net** Erla Zwingle's witty and eye-opening blog on life in Venice, including sobering accounts of how pickpockets operate.

Ⓦ **veneziablog.blogspot.co.uk** An excellent blog by a Venice-dwelling American-Italian who goes by the name of "Signor Nonloso".

Ⓦ **veneziaunica.it** This website is the place to go for info on the Venezia Unica passes, and the city's calendar of events.

Mon–Fri 8.20am–1.35pm, and Sat 8.20am–12.35pm. Stamps can usually be bought in *tabacchi*, as well as in some gift shops.

Public toilets

There are toilets on or very near most of the main squares, signposted by green and white "WC" stickers on the walls or ground. You'll need to pay, but many toilets are staffed, so you can get change; note that there is an option on the Venice Unica Card (see page 138) to have free access to staffed toilets. The main facilities are at Piazzale Roma; in the Giardinetti Reali, by the main tourist office; off the west side of the Piazza; the train station; and on the west side of the Accademia bridge.

Telephones

To call Italy from abroad dial your international access code, followed by 39 for Italy, followed by the full Italian number. From direct international calls from Italy, dial the country code, the area code (minus its first 0), and finally the subscriber number. If you are in Italy for some time and decide to opt for an Italian SIM, one of the most

reasonably priced and straightforward operators is Ho (Ⓦ ho-mobile.it).

Time

Italy is on Central European Time (CET), which means that it is one hour ahead of the UK, six hours ahead of Eastern Standard Time and nine hours ahead of Pacific Standard Time.

Tipping

Tipping is appreciated rather than expected.

Tourist information

Venice's main **tourist office** is at Calle dell'Ascensione 71/F, in the corner of the Piazza's arcades (Ⓦ veneziaunica. it); this is also the main outlet for information on the rest of the Veneto. Another office is located at the train station. Smaller offices are in the airport arrivals area and at the multistorey car park at Piazzale Roma.

For up to date cultural information, one of the best resources is the English–Italian *VENews* (Ⓦ venezia news.it), with good coverage of exhibitions, cultural events, bars and restaurants.

Festivals and events

Carnevale

The ten days before Lent
Ⓦ carnivalofvenice.com.
John Evelyn wrote of the 1646 Carnevale: "all the world was in Venice to see the folly and madness... the women, men and persons of all conditions disguising themselves in antique dresses, & extravagant Musique & a thousand gambols". Not much is different in today's Carnevale, for which people arrive in such numbers that the causeway from the mainland has sometimes had to be closed because the city is too packed. Originating as a communal party prior to the abstemious rigours of Lent, Carnevale takes place over ten days, finishing on Shrove Tuesday with a masked ball for the glitterati, and dancing in the Piazza for the plebs. During the day people parade in costumes on the Piazza; parents dress up their kids; businessmen can be seen doing their shopping in the classic white mask, black cloak and tricorne hat. In the evening some congregate in the remoter squares, while those in elaborate costumes install themselves in the windows of *Florian*. But you don't necessarily need to spend much money: a simple black outfit and a painted face is enough to transform you from a spectator into a participant.

La Sensa

May, Sun after Ascension Day
The feast of La Sensa happens on the Sunday after Ascension Day – the latter being the day on which the doge enacted the wedding of Venice to the sea. The ritual has recently been revived – a distinctly feeble procession which ends with the mayor and a gang of other dignitaries getting into a present-day approximation of the *Bucintoro* (the state barge) and sailing off to the Lido. A gondola regatta follows the ceremony.

Vogalonga

Second Sun after Ascension
Far more spectacular than La Sensa is the Vogalonga ("long row"), which is held a week later. Established in 1974 as a protest against the excessive number of motorboats on the canals, the Vogalonga is now open to any crew in any class of rowing boat, and covers a 32km course from the Bacino di San Marco to Burano and back; the competitors set off at 8.30am and arrive at the bottom of the Canal Grande anywhere between about 11am & 3pm.

The Biennale

June–Nov, odd numbered years
Ⓦ labiennale.org.
The Venice Biennale, Europe's most glamorous international forum for contemporary art, was inaugurated in 1895 and is now held every odd-numbered year from June to November. The main site is by the Giardini Pubblici, with permanent pavilions for about forty countries plus space for a thematic international exhibition. This core part is supplemented by exhibitions in parts of the Arsenale that are otherwise closed to the public, such as the colossal Corderie or Tana (the former rope-factory). Various sites throughout the city (eg salt warehouses on the Záttere) are used as national pavilions and as venues for fringe exhibitions. Some of the Biennale pavilions and other buildings (usually the Tana) are used in even-numbered years for an independent Biennale for architecture, a smaller event which runs from the second week of September to mid-November; this overlaps with a brief music Biennale, and is preceded by a two-week dance Biennale.

National holidays

Many fee-charging sights (but not bars and restaurants) close on the following dates: **January 1**; **January 6** (Epiphany); **Easter Monday**; **April 25** (Liberation Day and St Mark's Day); **May 1** (Labour Day); **June 2** (Day of the Republic); **August 15** (Assumption of the Blessed Virgin Mary); **November 1** (Ogni Santi, "All Saints"); **December 8** (Immaculate Conception of the Blessed Virgin Mary); **December 25**; **December 26**. Many Venetian shops and businesses also close or work shorter hours for the local festival of the Salute on **November 21**.

Festa del Redentore

Third Sun in July

The Festa del Redentore is one of Venice's plague-related festivals, marking the end of the 1576 epidemic. The day centres on Palladio's church of the Redentore, which was built by way of thanksgiving. A bridge of boats is strung across the Giudecca canal to allow the faithful to walk over to the church, and on the preceding Saturday night hundreds of people row out for a picnic on the water. The night ends with fireworks, after which it's traditional to row to the Lido for sunrise.

The Film Festival

Eleven days in late Aug and/or early Sept ⓦ labiennale.org.

The Venice Film Festival (Mostra Internazionale d'Arte Cinematografica), founded in 1932, is the world's oldest. The eleven-day event takes place on the Lido. The main screen is the **Palazzo del Cinemà**, next to the *Excelsior* hotel on Lungomare G. Marconi; other screenings take place in the vast **PalaBiennale** marquee, the four-screen **Palazzo del Casinò**, and the **Sala Darsena**. Tickets are available to the public on the day before the performance, at the Palazzo del Cinemà and PalaBiennale ticket offices and at the Biennale HQ, just west of the Piazza at Calle del Ridotto 1365a.

The Regata Storica

First Sun in Sept

The Regata Storica is the annual trial of strength and skill for the city's gondoliers and other expert rowers. It starts with a procession of richly decorated historic craft along the Canal Grande, their crews all decked out in period dress, followed by a series of races right up the canal. Re-enacting the return of Caterina Cornaro to her native city in 1489, the opening parade is spectacular. The first race of the day is for young rowers in two-oared *pupparini*; the women's race comes next (in boats called *mascarete*), followed by a race for canoe-like *caorline*; and then it's the big one – the men's race, in specialized two-man racing gondolas called *gondolini*.

La Salute

Nov 21

The Festa della Salute is a reminder of the 1630–31 plague, which killed one-third of the lagoon's population. The Salute church was built in thanks for deliverance from the outbreak, and since then the Venetians have processed over a pontoon bridge across the Canal Grande to give thanks for their health, or to pray for the sick. It offers the only chance to see the church as it was designed to be seen – with its main doors open and hundreds of people milling up and down the steps.

Chronology

453 The first mass migration into the Venetian lagoon is provoked by the incursions of Attila the Hun's hordes.

568 Permanent settlement is accelerated when the Germanic Lombards (or Longobards) sweep into northern Italy. The resulting confederation owes political allegiance to Byzantium.

726 The lagoon settlers choose their first doge, Orso Ipato.

810 After the Frankish army of Charlemagne has overrun the Lombards, the emperor's son Pepin sails into action against the proto-Venetians and is defeated. The lagoon settlers withdraw to the better-protected islands of Rivoalto, the name by which the central cluster of islands was known until the late twelfth century, when it became generally known as Venice.

828 The Venetians signal their independence through a great symbolic act – the theft of the body of St Mark from Alexandria. St Mark is made the patron saint of the city, and a basilica is built alongside the doge's castle to accommodate the holy relics.

1000 A fleet commanded by Doge Pietro Orseolo II subjugates the Slav pirates who have been impeding Venetian trade in the northern Adriatic. The expedition is commemorated annually in the ceremony of the Marriage of Venice to the Sea.

1081 The Byzantine emperor Alexius Comnenus appeals to Venice for aid against the Normans of southern Italy. In the following year the emperor declares Venetian merchants to be exempt from all tolls and taxes within his lands. In the words of one historian – "On that day Venetian world trade began".

1095 The commencement of the First Crusade. Offering to transport armies and supplies to the East in return for grants of property and financial bonuses, Venice extends its foothold in the Aegean, the Black Sea and Syria.

1177 Having been embroiled in the political manoeuvrings between the papacy, the Western Emperor and the cities of northern Italy, Venice brings off one of its greatest diplomatic successes: the reconciliation of Emperor Frederick Barbarossa and Pope Alexander III.

1204 Venice plays a major role in the Fourth Crusade and the Sack of Constantinople. Thousands are massacred by the Christian soldiers and virtually every precious object that can be lifted is stolen from the city, mainly by the Venetians, who now have an almost uninterrupted chain of ports stretching from the lagoon to the Black Sea.

1297 The passing of the Serrata del Maggior Consiglio, a measure which basically allows a role in the government of the city only to those families already involved in it. The Serrata is to remain in effect, with minimal changes, until the end of the Venetian Republic five centuries later.

1310 Following an uprising led by Bajamonte Tiepolo, the Council of Ten is created to supervise internal security.

1355 Doge Marin Falier is executed, after plotting to overthrow the councils of Venice and install himself as absolute ruler.

1380 Almost a century of sporadic warfare against Genoa – Venice's chief commercial rival in the eastern Mediterranean – climaxes with the War of Chioggia. The invading Genoese are driven out of the lagoon, and it soon becomes clear that Venice has at last won the tussle for economic and political supremacy.

1420 Venice annexes Friuli and Udine, which were formerly ruled by the King of Hungary, virtually doubling the area of its *terra firma* (mainland) empire, extending it right up to the Alps.

1441 Doge Francesco Fóscari, having led Venice against Filippo Maria Visconti of Milan, signs the Treaty of Cremona, which confirms Venetian control of Peschiera, Brescia, Bergamo and part of the territory of Cremona.

1453 Constantinople falls to the Turkish army of Sultan Mahomet II, which results in the erosion of Venice's commercial empire in the East.

1494 Italy is invaded by Louis XII of France. In the ensuing chaos Venice succeeds in adding bits and pieces to its *terra firma* domain, but when it begins to encroach on papal territory in Romagna, it provokes – in 1508 – the formation of the League of Cambrai, with Pope Julius II, Louis XII, Emperor Maximilian and the King of Spain at its head.

1499 The defeat of the Venetian navy at Sapienza leads to the loss of the main fortresses of the Morea (Peloponnese), which means that the Turks now control the so-called "door to the Adriatic".

1516 End of the War of the League of Cambrai. Venice still possesses nearly everything it held at the start of the war, but many of the cities of

the Veneto have been sacked and the Venetian treasury bled almost dry.

1519 With the accession of the 19-year-old Charles V, the Habsburg Empire absorbs the massive territories of the Spanish kingdom, and the whole Italian peninsula, with the sole exception of Venice, is soon under the emperor's domination.

1571 The Venetian fleet is instrumental in the defeat of the Turks at Lépanto, but in subsequent negotiations Venice is forced to surrender Cyprus.

1606 Friction between the papacy and Venice comes to a head with a Papal Interdict and the excommunication of the whole city.

1669 Prolonged Turkish harassment of the Venetian colonies culminates with the fall of Crete.

1699 Under the command of Doge Francesco Morosini, the Venetians embark on a retaliatory action in the Morea (Peloponnese), and succeed in retaking the region, albeit for only a short time.

1718 In the Treaty of Passarowitz Venice is forced to accept a definition of its Mediterranean empire drawn up by the Austrians and the Turks. It is left with just the Ionian islands and the Dalmatian coast, and its power in these colonies is little more than hypothetical.

1748 By now a political nonentity, Venice signs the Treaty of Aix-la-Chapelle, which confirms Austrian control of what had once been Venice's mainland empire.

1797 Having mollified the Austrians by handing over the Veneto to them,

Napoleon waits for a pretext to polish off the Republic itself. On April 20, the Venetians attack a French naval patrol off the Lido. On May 9 an ultimatum is sent to the city's government, demanding the dissolution of its constitution. On Friday, May 12, 1797, the Maggior Consiglio (in effect the city's parliament) meets for the last time, voting to accede to Napoleon's demands. The Venetian Republic is dead. By the Treaty of Campo Formio, Napoleon relinquishes Venice to the Austrians.

1805 Napoleon joins the city to his Kingdom of Italy, and it stays under French domination until the aftermath of Waterloo.

1815 Venice passes back to the Austrians, and remains a Habsburg province for the next half-century, the only break in Austrian rule coming with the revolt of March 1848, when the city is reinstituted as a republic under the leadership of Daniele Manin. The rebellion lasts until August 1849.

1866 Venice is absorbed into the Kingdom of United Italy.

1869 The opening of the Suez Canal brings a muted revival to the shipbuilders of Venice's Arsenale, but tourism is now emerging as the main area of economic expansion, with the development of the Lido as Europe's most fashionable resort.

1917 The navy dismantles the Arsenale and switches its yards to Genoa and Naples.

1933 Venice Is joined to the mainland as a road link is built to carry workers between Venice and the steadily expanding refineries and factories of Porto Marghera. Rapid depopulation of the historic centre soon follows, as workers decamp to Mestre, where housing is drier, roomier, warmer and cheaper.

2003 With the number of annual *acque alte* (floods) exceeding one hundred, in April 2003 work begins on the construction of the tidal barrier (see page 119).

2005 Massimo Cacciari elected mayor for a second term and tries to persuade the local administration and conservation groups to focus on residential property instead of churches and monuments. Gentrification and rehabilitation of areas such as Giudecca and Sant'Elena begins.

2008 The population of the historic centre of Venice falls below sixty thousand. The annual number of tourist visits now exceeds twenty million; tourism generates around seventy percent of the city's income.

2019 The worst floods ever recorded hit the city in November, after a decade in which the frequency of dangerously high acque alte (i.e 140cm or more over the mean) increases. Partly a result of sea level rises and the climate crisis, partly because of massive changes that land reclamation and deep-ship canal schemes have made to the structure of the lagoon.

2020 The flood barrier opens in October. It is effective as long as weather events are predictable but takes hours to rise into place, and in December 2020 sudden storms push the water over the barrier causing severe floods.

2023 Population of Venice's *centro storico* is 51,000 – less than a third of the population of 1945.

Italian

What follows is a brief pronunciation guide and a rundown of essential words and phrases. For more detail, see the *Italian: Rough Guide Phrasebook*.

Pronunciation

Italian **pronunciation** is easy, since every word is spoken exactly as it is written, with only a few **consonants** that are different from English:

c before e or i i is pronounced as in **ch**urch; **ch** before the same vowels is hard, as in **c**at.

sci or **sce** are pronounced as in **she**et and **she**lter respectively.

g is soft before **e** and **i**, as in **g**eranium; hard when followed by **h**, as in **g**arlic.

gn has the ni sound of our "o**ni**on".

gl in Italian is softened to something like li in English, as in stal**li**on.

h is not aspirated, as in **h**onour.

Italian words are stressed on the penultimate syllable unless an **accent** (´ or `) denotes otherwise, although written accents are often left out in practice. Note that the ending –ia or –ie counts as two syllables, hence *trattoria* is stressed on the **i**.

Words and phrases

Basics

Good morning Buon giorno
Good afternoon/evening Buona sera
Good night Buona notte
Goodbye Arrivederci
Yes Sì
No No
Please Per favore
Thank you (very much) Grazie (molte/mille grazie)
You're welcome Prego
Alright/that's OK Va bene
How are you? Come stai/sta? (informal/formal)
I'm fine Bene
Do you speak English? Parla inglese?
I don't understand Non ho capito
I don't know Non lo so
Excuse me Mi scusi/Prego
Excuse me (in a crowd) Permesso
I'm sorry Mi dispiace
I'm English Sono inglese
...Scottish ...scozzese
...American ...americano
...Irish ...irlandese
...Welsh ...gallese
Today Oggi
Tomorrow Domani
Day after tomorrow Dopodomani
Yesterday Ieri
Now Adesso
Later Più tardi
Wait a minute! Aspetta!
In the morning Di mattina
In the afternoon Nel pomeriggio
In the evening Di sera
Here/there Qui/Là
Good/bad Buono/Cattivo
Big/small Grande/Piccolo
Cheap/expensive Economico/Caro
Hot/cold Caldo/Freddo
Near/far Vicino/Lontano
Vacant/occupied Libero/Occupato
With/without Con/Senza
More/less Più/Meno
Enough, no more Basta
Mr... Signor...
Mrs... Signora...
Miss... Signorina... (il Signor, la Signora, la Signorina when speaking about someone else)

Some signs

Entrance/exit Entrata/Uscita
Open/closed Aperto/Chiuso
Arrivals/departures Arrivi/Partenze
Closed for restoration Chiuso per restauro
Closed for holidays Chiuso per ferie
Pull/push Tirare/Spingere
Beware Attenzione
No smoking Vietato fumare

Numbers

1 uno
2 due

3 tre
4 quattro
5 cinque
6 sei
7 sette
8 otto
9 nove
10 dieci
11 undici
12 dodici
13 tredici
14 quattordici
15 quindici
16 sedici
17 diciassette
18 diciotto
19 diciannove
20 venti
21 ventuno
22 ventidue
30 trenta
40 quaranta
50 cinquanta
60 sessanta
70 settanta
80 ottanta
90 novanta
100 cento
101 centuno
110 centodieci
200 duecento
500 cinquecento
1000 mille
5000 cinquemila

Transport

Ferry Traghetto
Bus station Autostazione
Train station Stazione ferroviaria
A ticket to... Un biglietto a...
One-way/return Solo andata/andata e ritorno
What time does it leave? A che ora parte?
Where does it leave from? Da dove parte?

Accommodation

Hotel Albergo
Do you have a room Ha una camera
...for one/two/three people ...per una/due/tre person(a/e)

...for one/twonights ...per una/due nott(e/i)
...with a double bed? ...con un letto matrimoniale?
...shower/bath ...doccia/bagno
Is breakfast included? È compresa la prima colazione?
I'll take it La prendo
I have a booking Ho una prenotazione
Youth hostel Ostello per la gioventù

In the restaurant

A table Una tavola
I'd like to book a table for two people at 8pm Vorrei prenotare una tavola per due alle otto
We need a knife Abbiamo bisogno di un coltello
a fork una forchetta
a spoon un cucchiaio
a glass un bicchiere
What do you recommend? Che cosa mi consiglia lei?
Waiter/waitress! Cameriere/a!
Bill/check Il conto
Is service included È incluso il servizio?
I'm a vegetarian Sono vegetariano/a
I'm a vegan Sono vegano/a
Gluten free Senza glutine

Questions and directions

Where? Dove?
Where is/are...? Dov'è/Dove sono?
When? Quando?
What? (What is it?) Cosa? (Cos'è?)
How much/many? Quanto/Quanti?
Why? Perché?
It is/There is (is it/is there...?) È/C'è (È/C'è...?)
What time is it? Che ora è/Che ore sono?
How do I get to...? Come arrivo a...?
What time does it open/close? A che ora apre/chiude?
How much does it/they cost? Quanto costa/costano?

Menu reader

Basics and snacks

Aceto Vinegar
Aglio Garlic

Biscotti Biscuits
Burro Butter
Cioccolato Chocolate
Formaggio Cheese
Frittata Omelette
Grissini Bread sticks
Marmellata Jam
Olio Oil
Olive Olives
Pane Bread
Pane integrale Wholemeal bread
Panino Bread roll
Patatine Crisps
Patatine fritte Chips
Pepe Pepper
Pizzetta Small cheese-and-tomato pizza
Riso Rice
Sale Salt
Tramezzino Sandwich (in crustless white bread)
Uova Eggs
Yogurt Yoghurt
Zucchero Sugar
Zuppa Soup

Starters (antipasti)

Antipasto misto Mixed cold meats and cheese (and other starters)
Caponata Mixed aubergine, olives, tomatoes and celery
Caprese Tomato and mozzarella salad
Insalata di mare Seafood salad
Insalata di riso Rice salad
Parmigiana Fried aubergine in tomato and parmesan cheese
Mortadella Salami-type cured meat
Pancetta Bacon
Peperonata Grilled peppers stewed in olive oil
Pomodori ripieni Stuffed tomatoes
Prosciutto Ham
Salame Salami

Soups

Brodo Clear broth
Minestre Any light soup
Minestrone Thick vegetable soup
Pasta e fagioli Pasta soup with beans
Pastina in brodo Pasta pieces in clear broth
Stracciatella Broth with egg

Pasta sauces

Aglio e olio (e peperoncino) Garlic and olive oil (and hot chillies)
Arrabbiata Spicy tomato sauce
Bolognese Meat sauce
Burro e salvia Butter and sage
Carbonara Cream, ham and beaten egg
Frutta di mare Seafood
Funghi Mushroom
Amatriciana Pork and tomato
Panna Cream
Parmigiano Parmesan cheese
Pomodoro Tomato sauce
Ragù Meat sauce
Vóngole Clam and tomato

Meat (carne)

Agnello Lamb
Bistecca Steak (the cut, not necessarily beef)
Coniglio Rabbit
Costolette Chops
Cotolette Cutlets
Fegatini Chicken livers
Fegato Liver
Involtini Steak slices, rolled and stuffed
Lingua Tongue
Maiale Pork
Manzo Beef
Ossobuco Shin of veal
Pollo Chicken
Polpette Meatballs
Rognoni Kidneys
Salsiccia Sausage
Saltimbocca Veal with ham
Spezzatino Stew
Tacchino Turkey
Trippa Tripe
Vitello Veal

Fish (pesce) and shellfish (crostacei)

Acciughe Anchovies
Anguilla Eel
Aragosta Lobster
Baccalà Dried salted cod
Bronzino/Branzino Sea-bass
Calamari Squid
Cape lungue Razor clams
Cape sante Scallops
Caparossoli Shrimps

Coda di rospo Monkfish
Cozze Mussels
Dentice Dentex (like sea-bass)
Gamberetti Shrimps
Gamberi Prawns
Granchio Crab
Merluzzo Cod
Orata Bream
Ostriche Oysters
Pescespada Swordfish
Polipo Octopus
Ricci di mare Sea urchins
Rombo Turbot
San Pietro John Dory
Sarde Sardines
Schie Shrimps
Seppie Cuttlefish
Sogliola Sole
Tonno Tuna
Triglie Red mullet
Trota Trout
Vongole Clams

Vegetables (contorni) and salad (insalata)

Asparagi Asparagus
Basílico Basil
Broccoli Broccoli
Capperi Capers
Carciofi Artichokes
Carciofini Artichoke hearts
Carotte Carrots
Cavolfiori Cauliflower
Cavolo Cabbage
Ceci Chickpeas
Cetriolo Cucumber
Cipolla Onion
Fagioli Beans
Fagiolini Green beans
Finocchio Fennel
Funghi Mushrooms
Insalata verde/insalata mista Green salad/mixed salad
Melanzana Aubergine/eggplant
Origano Oregano
Patate Potatoes
Peperoni Peppers
Piselli Peas
Pomodori Tomatoes
Radicchio Chicory

Spinaci Spinach
Zucca Pumpkin
Zucchini Courgettes

Desserts (dolci)

Cassata Ice-cream cake with candied fruit
Gelato Ice cream
Macedonia Fruit salad
Torta Cake, tart
Zabaglione Dessert made with eggs, sugar and Marsala wine
Zuppa Inglese Trifle

Fruit (frutta) and nuts (noce)

Ananas Pineapple
Anguria/Coccómero Watermelon
Arance Banane Bananas
Ciliegie Cherries
Fichi Figs
Fichi d'India Prickly pears
Fragole Strawberries
Limone Lemon
Mándorle Almonds
Mele Apples
Melone Melon
Pere Pears
Pesche Peaches
Pignoli Pine nuts
Uva Grapes

Drinks (bevande)

Acqua minerale Mineral water
Aranciata Orangeade
Bicchiere Glass
Birra Beer
Bottiglia Bottle
Caffè Coffee
Cioccolata calda Hot chocolate
Ghiaccio Ice
Granita Iced coffee or fruit drink
Latte Milk
Limonata Lemonade
Selz Soda water
Spremuta Fresh fruit juice
Spumante Sparkling wine
Succo Fruit juice with sugar
Tè Tea
Tonico Tonic water
Vino Wine
Rosso Red

Bianco White
Rosato Rosé
Secco Dry
Dolce Sweet
Litro Litre
Mezzo Half
Quarto Quarter
Salute! Cheers!

Venetian specialities

Antipasti e Primi (first course)

Acciughe marinate Marinated anchovies with onions
Bigoli in salsa Spaghetti with butter, onions and sardines
Brodetto Mixed fish soup, often with tomatoes and garlic
Castraura Artichoke hearts
Granseola alla Veneziana Crab cooked with oil, parsley and lemon
Pasta e fagioli Pasta and beans
Prosciutto San Daniele The best-quality prosciutto
Risotto alla sbirraglia Risotto with chicken, ham and vegetables
Risotto alla trevigiana Butter, onions andchicory risotto

Risotto di cape Risotto with clams and shellfish
Risotto di mare Seafood risotto
Sopa de peoci Mussel soup with garlic and parsley

Secondi (second course)

Anguilla alla Veneziana Eel cooked with lemon and tuna
Baccalà mantecato Salt cod simmered in milk
Fegato veneziana Sliced calf's liver cooked in olive oil with onion
Peoci salati Mussels with parsley and garlic
Risi e bisi Rice and peas, with parmesan and ham
Sarde in saor Marinated sardines
Seppie in nero Squid cooked in its ink
Seppioline nere Baby cuttlefish cooked in its ink

Dolci (Desserts)

Frittole alla Veneziana Rum and anise flavoured fritters filled with pine nuts, raisins and candied fruit
Tiramisù Layered dessert of savoiardi biscuits dipped in coffee and/or rum, and a mixture of mascarpone, egg yolks and sugar, dusted with cocoa

Publishing Information
Fourth edition 2024

Distribution

UK, Ireland and Europe
Apa Publications (UK) Ltd; sales@roughguides.com
United States and Canada
Ingram Publisher Services; ips@ingramcontent.com
Australia and New Zealand
Booktopia; retailer@booktopia.com.au
Worldwide
Apa Publications (UK) Ltd; sales@roughguides.com

Special Sales, Content Licensing and CoPublishing
Rough Guides can be purchased in bulk quantities at discounted prices. We can
create special editions, personalised jackets and corporate imprints tailored to
your needs. sales@roughguides.com.
roughguides.com

Printed in Czech Republic

This book was produced using **Typefi** automated publishing software.

A catalogue record for this book is available from the British Library

The publishers and authors have done their best to ensure the accuracy and
currency of all the information in **Pocket Rough Guide Venice**, however, they can
accept no responsibility for any loss, injury, or inconvenience sustained by any
traveller as a result of information or advice contained in the guide.

Rough Guide credits
Project editor: Joanna Reeves
Copy editor: Annie Warren
Cartography: Katie Bennett
Picture Editor: Piotr Kala
Picture Manager: Tom Smyth
Layout: Grzegorz Madejak
Original design: Richard Czapnik
Head of DTP and Pre-Press:
Rebeka Davies
Head of Publishing: Sarah Clark

About the author

Ros Belford is the author of *Children of the Volcano* (June 2024) a memoir about bringing her daughters up on a small Sicilian island. She has been travelling around and living in Italy since she was 18 years old and has written numerous guides to the country for Rough Guides and articles for publications ranging from *The Telegraph* to *Conde Nast Traveller*. Returning to Venice after twenty years' absence to update this book rekindled her passion for the most extraordinary city on earth.

Acknowledgements

Thank you to Venissa for the most thought-provoking lunch and wine-tastings I have ever experienced, to the *Belmond Cipriani* for showing what true luxury can be, and to everyone I met in Venice who is dedicated to discovering ways in which to make travel to the city sustainable.

Help us update

We've gone to a lot of effort to ensure that this edition of the **Pocket Rough Guide Venice** is accurate and up-to-date. However, things change – places get "discovered", opening hours are notoriously fickle, restaurants and rooms raise prices or lower standards. If you feel we've got it wrong or left something out, we'd like to know, and if you can remember the address, the price, the hours, the phone number, so much the better.

Please send your comments with the subject line "**Pocket Rough Guide Venice Update**" to mail@uk.roughguides.com. We'll credit all contributions and send a copy of the next edition (or any other Rough Guide if you prefer) for the very best emails.

Photo Credits

(Key: T-top; C-centre; B-bottom; L-left; R-right)

Alberto Valese 46
iStock 5, 12B, 13C, 14B, 14T, 15T, 16T, 20T, 21T, 21C, 21B, 28, 29, 30, 32, 36, 64, 70, 94, 95, 100, 111, 118
Martin Richardson/Rough Guides 87
Michelle Grant/Rough Guides 18T, 18C, 18B, 19B, 20B, 31, 47, 60, 82
Paolo della Corte/Antiche Carampane 73
Public domain 11B, 19T

Punta della Dogana 51
Shutterstock 1, 2T, 2BL, 2C, 2BR, 4, 6, 10, 11T, 12/13T, 12/13B, 15B, 16B, 17T, 17B, 19C, 20C, 22/23, 24, 27, 34, 35, 39, 40, 41, 43, 44, 49, 53, 54, 56, 59, 63, 67, 69, 75, 77, 78, 81, 84, 85, 89, 90, 91, 93, 97, 98, 104, 105, 106, 107, 108, 112, 113, 114, 115, 117, 121, 122, 124/125, 134/135
Venissa 116

Cover: Gondolas moored by Saint Mark's Square **Shutterstock**

Index

classical music
    Teatro Malibran 85
classical music (by area)
    Cannaregio 85
Crime and emergencies 141

D

directory A–Z 140
Discount passes 141
Dogana di Mare 105
Dorsoduro 48

E

Eastern Castello 94
electricity 142
Embassies and consulates
    142

F

festivals and events 145
    Carnevale 145
    Festa del Redentore 146
    La Salute 146
    La Sensa 145
    The Biennale 145
    The Film Festival 146
    The Regata Storica 146
    Vogalonga 145
Flooding and the barrier 119
Fondaco dei Tedeschi 106
Fondaco dei Turchi 101
Fondamente Nove 81

G

getting around 137
gondolas 52, 139

H

Health 142
hospital 142
hostels
    Combo Venice 132
    Domus Civica 132
    Foresteria Valdese 132
    Generator Hostel 132
    Ostello Santa Fosca 133

I

Il Gobbo 63
Il Redentore 120
internet access 142

L

La Fenice 41
La Giudecca 119
La Giudecca and San Giorgio
    Maggiore 118
La Pietà 91
left luggage 142
LGBTQ+ travellers 142
lost property 142

M

Madonna dell'Orto 78
maps
    Burano and Torcello 112
    Canal Grande 102
    Cannaregio 76
    Central Castello 88
    Dorsoduro 50
    Eastern Castello 96
    La Giudecca and San Giorgio
        Maggiore 120
    Murano 110
    Piazza San Marco 26
    San Marco: north of the
        Piazza 36
    San Marco: west of the
        Piazza 42
    San Pietro and Sant Elena
        Castello 98
    San Polo and Santa Croce 64
    Venice at a glance 8
Marco Polo airport 136
money 142
Murano 109
museums and monuments 142

N

national holidays 146

O

Opening hours 143
opera
    La Fenice 47
opera (by area)
    San Marco west of the Piazza 47
Oratorio dei Crociferi 81

P

Palazzi Barbaro 107
Palazzo Balbi 104
Palazzo Contarini-Fasan 107
Palazzo Corner della Ca'
    Grande 107

Palazzo Corner della Regina 104
Palazzo Dario 105
Palazzo dei Camerlenghi 104
Palazzo Farsetti 106
Palazzo Franchetti 107
Palazzo Grassi 44, 107
Palazzo Grimani 89, 106
Palazzo Labia 75, 105
Palazzo Loredan 106
Palazzo Mocenigo 66
Palazzo Querini-Stampalia 89
Palazzo Vendramin-Calergi 105
Palazzo Venier dei Leoni 104
Piazza San Marco 24
post offices 143
public toilets 144

R

restaurants
    Acquastanca 115
    Ai Mercanti 38
    Ai Promessi Sposi 82
    Ai Quattro Feri 60
    Al Bacareto 46
    Al Covo 99
    Al Gatto Nero 115
    Alla Fontana 82
    Alla Palanca 123
    Alla Vedova 83
    Alle Testiere 92
    Al Storico da Crea 123
    Anice Stellato 83
    Antiche Carampane 72
    Antico Dolo 72
    Bancogiro 72
    Bisicchia 60
    CHICheria 92
    Cip's 123
    Corte Sconta 99
    CoVino 99
    Da Carla 46
    Da Fiore 46
    Da Remigio 92
    Da Rioba 83
    Da Romano 116
    Da Valentino 99
    Gam Gam 83
    Harry's Bar 46
    Hostaria Bacanera 83
    Il Ridotto 93
    La Bitta 60
    La Calcina 60
    La Perla ai Bisatei 116
    Le Bistrot de Venise 39
    Majer 123
    Marcianino 83